Medjugorje Journal
Mary Speaks to the World

Medjugorje Journal
Mary Speaks to the World

Lucy Rooney, SND
Robert Faricy, SJ

McCRIMMONS
Great Wakering Essex

For Our Lady of Peace

Dedicated to
Sister Emmanuel Bali, OSU
our friend in the Lord Jesus

First published in 1987 by McCrimmon Publishing Co Ltd
Great Wakering, Essex, England

ISBN 0 85597 398 6

Cum permissu superiorum

All the photographs in this book, except those on pages 34,
89, 98, 117 and 144, are © by don Filippo Paravicini.

Cover design by Studio Reprographics
Picture © by F C Ferriere BA (Hons) Arch
Typesetting by Barry Sarling, Rayleigh, Essex
Printed by Mayhew McCrimmon Printers Ltd
Great Wakering, Essex

Contents

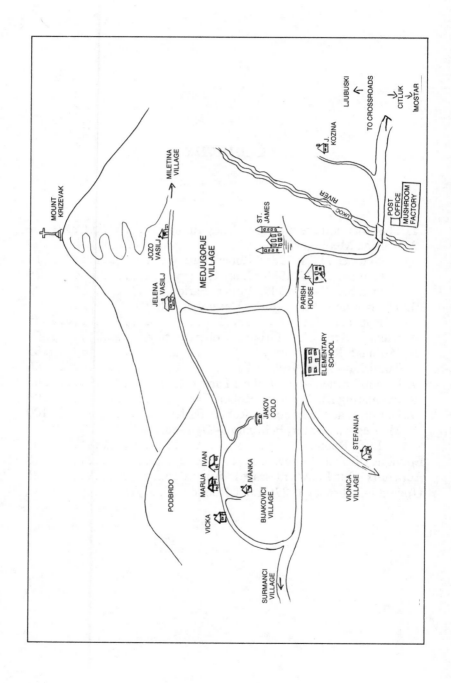

1. The story and the message

by Lucy Rooney

During the winter of 1985-86, Father Bob Faricy lived at Medjugorje. This book contains his personal journal, and also the journal of other visits that both he and I made to Medjugorje. In this chapter I want to set out briefly the facts of the Medjugorje story, and describe in broad outline the story's setting.

The setting

Christmas Day 1985 was a normal working day in Bosnia-Herce-govina. The Yugoslav communist government does not acknowledge Christmas; so the school bus left Medjugorje as usual at 6.20 am, taking the older pupils to their classes at Mostar, an hour's journey distant. Most of the Medjugorje boys and girls are Catholic, but in Mostar they share their studies with Muslims and Orthodox.

Back in the village, though the primary school was open, its desks were empty. By common consent all the small children remained at home. According to the Yugoslav constitution, religion is free; but it must be private.

The country we call Yugoslavia was set up on December 1, 1918, as a nation of South Slavs, that is, of Croats, Serbs and Slovenes. In its short history as a modern state it has been a constitutional monarchy, a land invaded, occupied and divided between Germany and Italy, while torn at the same time by civil war. Now it is a federal people's republic ruled by the League of Communists of Yugoslavia.

There are six federal republics in the union, together with two autonomous provinces. Amazingly, Yugoslavia hangs together, despite having six nationalities, three chief languages, three main

YUGOSLAVIA

religions and two alphabets. But increasingly, the six republics — Serbia, Croatia, Slovenia, Bosnia-Hercegovina, Montenegro and Macedonia — and the provinces of Vojvodina and Kosovo, become more protective of their interests. In the census of 1981, more than 22 million people were registered, eight million being Serbs, over four million Croats, four million Muslims, and over one million each Slovenes and Macedonians, with half a million Montenegrans and several minor national groups. Yet of the 22 million, only 1.2 million described themselves as Yugoslavs.

Religiously, the Orthodox are a majority — eight million. Catholics are six million and Muslims four million. Religion and nationality are closely identified, so that in general the Slovenes and Croats are Catholics, and the Serbs, Montenegrans and Macedonians are Orthodox (see map). This significant division draws a line the length of the country, and divides Europe also. To the west are the areas of Yugoslavia with Catholic majorities, and the countries belonging historically to the Latin Church; to the east are the areas of the eastern Orthodox Churches. Astride this dividing line is Bosnia-Hercegovina, where the events described in this book are taking place. Bosnia-Hercegovina unites east and west, having 32 per cent Orthodox, 18 per cent Catholic, and moreover, two million Muslims — 40 per cent of Bosnian people.

It was to this uniquely placed region that the Blessed Virgin Mary came, to plead for reconciliation and peace.

The story

On a summer evening, June 24, 1981, Mirjana and Ivanka went for a walk from their village, Bijakovici. The road they took — a track only — led them past the hill Podbrdo. Away to their right they could see the church of St James, and behind it Mount Krizevac, surmounted by a cross. They could see the four other villages which together with Bijakovici make up the parish of Medjugorje. Distant mountains ring the wide plain.

Fifteen-year-old Ivanka was the first to see something unusual,

✝ Medjugorje

something shining on the hillside. A second look, and she saw a form she took to be Our Lady. But 16-year-old Mirjana would have none of it and drew her back to the village. Later they returned to gather the sheep, and this time both clearly saw the figure.

'It really was Our Lady,' Ivanka said afterwards. 'She held Jesus on her arm. I saw a crown on her head; she was wearing a beautiful long robe.'

The subsequent story has been told in many books: how they ran back to the village for Vicka; how Ivan joined them; and how, next day, Marija and Jakov were added to the group. Crowds gathered each evening until the police intervened. The clergy were anxious — some believing, some not. But the pastor, Father Jozo Zovko, OFM, organised prayers and an evening Mass in the church. During the autumn and winter Our Lady continued to appear. The hill being closed off, she appeared in the fields or in various houses.

Her reason? She had already said: 'I am the Virgin Mary.' Now she added: 'I am the Queen of Peace. I have come to reconcile all people.'

Father Jozo Zovko spent many hours praying for light to know what to do. One afternoon he was in church at prayer. 'I was in anguish,' he said later. 'I prayed: "God, I know you talked to Abraham, to Moses…There are thousands of people here, and I do not know the source of this river, nor where it is going." At that moment, a voice spoke: "Come out and protect the children".'

Father Jozo hastened out of the church and saw the six children racing towards him. 'Hide us!' they shouted. 'The police are chasing us!' He took them into the rectory, just in time. The police arrived, asking if he had seen the children. 'Yes,' he answered, and the police rushed on to Bijakovici. That was the first sign to the pastor, Father Jozo Zovko, that the apparitions were genuine.

Later that summer Our Lady appeared to him and to the children during the evening prayers in the church. She did not speak. Father Jozo was a changed man. But he knew the price. 'Be prepared to take my place,' he said to Father Tomislav Vlasic, who had been sent to help him. Soon, what he expected happened — a police raid on the parish. Father Jozo was arrested, tried for sedition and sentenced to three and a half years' imprisonment. But not before he had arranged for all the events on the hill to be brought to the church and centred on the Mass. The six children were to come each evening to a small room off the sanctuary. There Our Lady continued to appear to them until early 1985, when the bishop, Bishop Pavao Zanic, forbade them to have the visions in the church. Since then Our Lady has been appearing to them in the parish house.

Signs and secrets

The apocalyptic signs seen by many people at Medjugorje — the sun spinning, visions, fire and unexplained lights, the frequent references to Satan, the 10 secrets concerning future events, some of them catastrophic — have all drawn the world's attention. And that is precisely Our Lady's intention — to wake us up. There is a sense at Medjugorje of the imminence of the 'admonitions' which the Blessed Virgin has foretold. After these admonitions, Our Lady has said she will leave a permanent visible sign at the site of the first apparitions, to convert, if possible, even unbelievers.

Two of the young people have been given 10 secrets. When Ivanka received the tenth in 1985, Our Lady told her she would appear to her in future only on June 25 of each year. Mirjana's visions had ceased in 1982, except for her birthday each year. But Mirjana has been given a special role — that of responsibility for making the secrets known at the appointed time. During 1985 and 1986 she saw Our Lady and heard her voice a number of times on account of the secrets. Mirjana was to choose a priest to whom she would tell each secret 10 days before its fulfilment. She chose Father Pero Ljubicic, OFM. Father Pero will receive from Mirjana a document on which the secrets are written; a document which the Blessed Virgin has given to Mirjana. No one else can read it. Father Pero will have seven days to pray, and three days to announce to the world what is to happen.

Mirjana's eyes fill with tears when she remembers the first admonition to the world, which she has seen in a vision. She asked Our Lady: 'Does it have to be like that?' Our Lady replied: 'Look at the way the world is living.'

★ ★ ★

VICKA IVANKOVIC was born July 3, 1964. She has five sisters and two brothers. Vicka is forceful and practical, vivacious. Often she suffers severe headaches because of a non-malignant, but inoperable, cyst on the brain.

MIRJANA DRAGICEVIC was born March 18, 1965. Her family belong to Bijakovici; but they live in Sarajevo, where Mirjana is a student of agronomy. She has one brother.

MARIJA PAVLOVIC was born April 1, 1964. She has three brothers and two sisters. Marija has finished studying and lives at home, helping, when she can escape the crowds, with work in the fields and pasturing the sheep.

IVAN DRAGICEVIC was born May 25, 1965. He is the eldest of three boys. He worked on the land, after returning from a junior seminary where the studies were beyond him. He would still like to be a priest. In June 1986 Ivan was conscripted for military service.

IVANKA IVANKOVIC was born April 21, 1966. Though belonging to Bijakovici, she lives at Mostar with her father, one brother, one sister and her grandmother. Since her mother died, Ivanka has been keeping house.

JAKOV COLO was born June 3, 1971, and lives with his uncle and aunt and their small girls. Jakov's mother died in 1984; his father died in 1986. He goes to a secondary school at Citluk.

Another two girls who see Our Lady live not in Bijakovici but in Medjugorje village:

JELENA VASILJ was born May 14, 1972. Jelena is the second of six children. Since December 15, 1982, she has had inner locutions and, later, visions of Our Lady. She receives messages from the Blessed Virgin for two of the prayer groups.

MARIJANA VASILJ is no relation of Jelena. She was born October 5, 1971, one of five children. She began to experience inner locutions in March 1983, and later visions of Our Lady, at first interior, then exterior. A close friend of Jelena's, Marijana also receives messages from Our Lady for two of the three main prayer groups. Both Jelena and Marijana are at secondary school in Mostar.

2. Visiting Medjugorje

October 11-14, 1985 (Robert Faricy)

October 11, Friday. I arrived Thursday morning with Father Philip Pavich, an American Franciscan priest who speaks Croatian. His first visit here, my fifth. Last night, as she does every evening, Our Lady came to Ivan, Marija, and Jakov at 5.45 pm in the small room near the front door of the house where the Franciscan priests and sisters live. And as always she appeared as a young woman of the region, fully three-dimensional, like anyone else except that she stands a few feet above the floor. No one saw her, as usual, except Ivan, Marija, and Jakov. They all spoke together in Croatian. Every Thursday, the Blessed Virgin gives to Marija a message for the people of the parish. Here is the message she gave last night:

Dear children. Again today I want to call you to live out my messages in the parish. I want to call especially the young persons of the parish; I love this parish so much. Dear children, if you live my messages, you live the seed of holiness. As your mother, I want to call all of you to holiness so that you can lead others to holiness — because you are like a mirror for other people. Thank you for responding to my call.

After the 6 pm Mass, Father Slavko Barbaric read the message to the parish. Later, Father Dobroslav Stojic took Philip and me in the community car to our rooms with local families nearby — just over the little bridge near the church and down a side road. My room is with the family of Jokan Kozina, a quiet, pleasant man who has a small vineyard near the house.

This morning, praying in my room, I found myself distracted and praying poorly. Then, all of a sudden, it seemed that my room was

• *Rapt: Ivan, Jakov and Marija listen intently as Our Lady appears to them in the house of the priests and sisters. Watching them (right) is Fr Robert Faricy.*

• *Mirjana*

• *Ivanka*

filled with the presence of Our Lady. It's the kind of thing that happens here.

The local communist government of the town of Citluk has begun to move in on Medjugorje to make some money. The communists have built a shack near the church with the words in large letters, *Turist Biro* (Tourist Bureau). I asked the young girl who staffs the tourist bureau if she works for the church or the government. She looked abashed when she answered. The *Turist Biro* stands for the local government's presence in Medjugorje.

The government has imposed a different tax law for Citluk and for Medjugorje than for anywhere else. Normally the government tax on a person paying for overnight lodging and food is 800 dinar, or 1200 dinar at most (in Dubrovnik, for example). But in the Citluk area, it is 2100 dinar, about seven US dollars.

Over a hundred years ago, during the Turkish occupation of this region, the Turks imposed a 10 per cent tax on all income. The people of Hercegovina revolted. The present tax, much higher than 10 per cent, has precipitated a lot of grumbling, but no revolt.

Inspectors (tourist board officials), women usually, check to see that those who take in people pay their tax. Some of the locals get around this by registering their houses as boarder-taking homes not in Citluk through a Citluk hotel, as would be normal, but through a hotel in another town outside the Citluk area. They then pay the lower, normal, tax.

The police also check on homes to see if they have paying visitors whom the house-owners have not registered with the police. All who take roomers must register them with the Citluk police. The police fine violators heavily.

All this, of course, forms part of the general government harassment of the people of Medjugorje. The people seem to me extraordinarily patient with a government that taps their telephones, opens their mail, and taxes them exorbitantly because they claim Our Lady visits the parish.

There have been some changes in the Franciscan community here. Father Slavko Barbaric, who acted as spiritual director of the four young people who see and speak with Our Lady every evening, has been transferred by the Franciscan provincial, acting under severe pressure from the local bishop, Bishop Pavao Zanic of Mostar. The bishop, ferocious opponent and colourful debunker of the apparitions here, has been — they say — silenced by Rome. He no longer makes the violent public statements about Medjugorje that he used to. He made his last polemical statement in spring 1985 on prime-time Italian television. The Vatican had shown great tolerance for what the bishop had been saying in public, until he said it in Italian at 7 pm on Channel One of the Italian TV network. Bishop Zanic, of course, still exercises real jurisdiction over his diocese, which includes Medjugorje. He has determined to close down the operation, which he calls a hoax perpetrated by the Franciscans, and to stop all pilgrimages there. I can see why he wanted Slavko transferred.

Father Slavko speaks five languages fluently. A dynamic preacher and organiser, he acted as the sparkplug at Medjugorje. And he still does. Transferred to a parish in the village of Blagaj, only seven miles away, and given minimal ministerial duties, he comes to Medjugorje daily for almost the whole day, and continues to do what he did before: preach, speak to the various language groups about Our Lady and her message, help individual pilgrims, and in general animate spiritually the parish and the pilgrims.

The man Slavko replaced two years ago, Tomislav Vlasic, who was also moved under episcopal pressure, has recently been relieved of some of his duties at the parish in Vitina, about 15 miles away. He now spends much time at Medjugorje.

The result: Father Tomislav Vlasic has, at least partly, come back; Father Slavko has, for practical purposes, never left; and Medjugorje has gained a new priest, Father Ivan Dugandzic.

On September 19, Father Ivan replaced Father Slavko as spiritual director of the young people who meet daily with Our Lady. He is well qualified, with a doctorate in theology, important scholarly publications in mystical theology, nine years' experience as Master of Novices of the Franciscan Province here in Hercegovina, and constant contact with the events at Medjugorje. Moreover, he is one of the members, probably the best qualified, of the official commission appointed by Bishop Zanic to investigate all aspects of the Marian apparitions here.

Other changes here: Sister Melanija Sakota has left and been assigned to study nursing in Dubrovnik. This is a real loss, since she was particularly close to the young persons who see the Blessed Virgin, and because she actively assisted both Father Slavko and

Sister Janja Boras. Last night Sister Melanija, as beautiful as ever, came back to Medjugorje for a few days' vacation from her studies.

Father Tomislav Pervan continues as the pastor of the parish. Sister Janja still does all the things she did before: taking charge of meals, helping pilgrims, guiding the four young people, working in the religious goods store. Fathers Pero Ljubicic and Dobroslav Stoijc are both here. Father Pero works a lot with the pilgrims, and Father Dobroslav takes care of much of the regular parish ministry. Sister Ignacija Bebek still acts as head sacristan.

Sister Ana Cotic, a cheerful young sister, has come to replace Sister Melanija. She works with Sister Janja in the kitchen, helps clean the church at night, and cleans the parish house. She is 28 years old, tall and attractive, with the easy grace of a natural athlete. She moves like she's dancing to African drums. As I write this, she has come into the room to read the daily newspaper. She skips the headlines to read the sports page. She played centre forward on a men's soccer team before she entered the convent. She is, literally, in love with Jesus. And it shows.

I had a long conversation with Father Jozo Zovko, the pastor here at the time of the first apparitions in 1981. He was imprisoned by the communist government and served one and a half years of his sentence before being released only on condition that he never again be assigned to Medjugorje. He knows about suffering. In prison he had no book, not even a Bible; could not say Mass; and was tortured

• *Fr Tomislav Vlasic*   • *Fr Jozo Zovko*

(he says, euphemistically, 'They have ways of getting you to do what they want').

Father Jozo and I talked about various attitudes to the Medjugorje events. He insists that we should not aggressively defend the authenticity of these events. No need to 'prove the bishop wrong', nor to point fingers. We should, Jozo says, remain obedient and humble, carrying the crosses that the Lord sends. And there is no need for long-range planning. The Lord has his plan. He reveals it little by little. We can follow it humbly and obediently.

'How should we talk about Medjugorje?' says Jozo. 'On our knees! It's holy.' I listen to him talk, thinking how clearly touched by God he is.

I've begun to study Croatian. Discouraging. It looks impossible.

Vicka's illness seems worse and more mysterious than ever. Usually she does not come to the church for the rosary, the Mass, and the other prayers. And she does not come to the Franciscan house for the evening visit of Our Lady. In fact, the Blessed Virgin comes to Vicka at home at the same time that she visits the other three in the small front room of the parish house.

Vicka spends much time in bed, has frequent prolonged attacks of severe pain in her head, lapses often into a kind of coma during these attacks. The doctors examined her last week, but have recommended no medicine or treatment. Vicka says such suffering has real and great value for the salvation of souls. She does not ask the Lord to take it away. On the contrary, she regards it a privilege to suffer for him and to share in the work of redemption.

Marija helps Sister Ignacija in the sacristy after Mass. In the sacristy after the six o'clock Mass last night I spoke to her briefly in Italian. Her Italian is good. I told her I had begun to study Croatian, and she told me to say something besides, 'How are you?' and 'Fine, thank you.' But I couldn't think of anything that I could put into words.

Friday evening. When the joyful and sorrowful mysteries of the rosary begin at five o'clock, the church is already full. By 5.45, when Our Lady appears to the four young people in a small room in the house of the Franciscan priests and sisters, the crowd in the church has overflowed into the vestibule and on down the front steps. The aisles are solid with people standing. Even the front of the sanctuary right up to the altar and on both sides has filled with people standing, sitting, kneeling.

Mass begins at six. Many in the church, perhaps most, are pilgrims. Many Italians, some Germans, a group from France, Austrians, Americans, British, and others. Less than half the congregation can follow the Mass in Croatian and the long, powerfully delivered sermon. But you could hear a pin drop. No one stirs during the whole hour up to the time for Holy Communion.

After Mass and the (usual here) Creed, seven *Our Fathers,* seven *Hail Marys,* and seven *Glory be's,* Father Slavko announces that, as on every Friday evening, there will be adoration of the cross after the Mass. He speaks in Croatian, German and Italian. I make the same announcements in French and English, although Slavko speaks both quite well.

Then Fathers Slavko and Tomislav Pervan lead the adoration, kneeling on the altar steps. Many people have left, but the church is still completely full; many have to stand in the aisles or kneel on the altar steps.

The service is moving: spontaneous prayers by the two priests, interspersed with litany-type prayers in which Slavko prays for a minute or so and the congregation responds in a set and short formula. I understand nothing of the Croatian, until Tomislav Pervan prays a few minutes in English.

The service ends after almost an hour with the blessing of religious objects by the priests, and the singing of the *Salve Regina* in Latin. Almost everyone present apparently knows the hymn, and the singing is loud and full.

Today, like every Wednesday and Friday, has been a fast day. Most people in the village, and many of the pilgrims, fast on bread and water every Wednesday and every Friday. My first meal in the Kozina house will be breakfast tomorrow.

October 12, Saturday. Since Philip and I arrived the weather has been sunny, warm for October, with clear blue skies. Early morning and evening are cool, but by noon it's warm enough to go without a sweater.

Slavko has promised me a Xerox copy of a study he has done concerning Jelena and, to a lesser extent, Marijana. Jelena Vasilj and Marijana Vasilj, who are friends but not relatives, frequently see and speak with Our Lady. Not part of the regular group of young people, they apparently have a special place in Our Lady's plan for Medjugorje. They look to me like normal 13-year-old girls. But they do have extraordinary spiritual experiences. I'm looking forward to reading Slavko's study.

• *Jelena Vasilj and Marijana Vasilj.*

We priests hear confessions every day during the rosary before Mass, from 5 pm to just before 6 pm; then we go to the sacristy to vest for the concelebrated Mass. The four confessionals in the back of the church are used for confessions in Croatian. Outside, along the east side of the church, we foreign priests hear confessions in various languages: German, French, Italian, English, and other languages according to the need. I hear confessions in Italian, English, and French. Eight or ten of us priests sit in chairs along the side of the church, allowing adequate spaces between us for privacy. The people stand in lines in the dirt field alongside the church. Since there is not enough room along the outside church wall, several priests hear confessions sitting in chairs in the field. Last night, for instance, I saw Philip, Pero, and Ivan there.

Hearing confessions, especially here, really builds me up. People are so good, and so humble. At Medjugorje many conversions take place. Persons who have not been to confession for years come here and start over. It makes me feel quite small. A humbling experience for a priest.

The sacristy before Mass is chaotic with movement, but quite silent and prayerful. About 30 of us concelebrated last night, crowding the altar. All vesting together in a sacristy built for one priest makes a tight squeeze. As a matter of fact, there are not too many priests at Mass. We need them all to move out into the congregation, and even outside the church, to distribute Holy Communion.

Various groups use the church all day long. Right now, for example, as I write this in a rear pew, nine priests concelebrate Mass at the altar for a group of about 300 pilgrims. I do not recognise the language. It sounds like Slovenian. The ubiquitous Slavko plays the organ.

At other times of the day, Slavko speaks to groups of pilgrims in Italian or in German. Or Sister Janja speaks to English-speaking groups. They explain the message of Our Lady at Medjugorje, that she calls us to conversion, to faith, to prayer, to penance and fasting, and to pray for peace in the world.

Father Slavko and Sister Janja frequently take groups to the basement of the parish house to watch videotapes. They have several, in various languages, taken at different times by different groups. The best I have seen are by Father Ed Serena, of Boston; he comes frequently to takes lots of video footage, which he then carefully edits in Boston to produce the videotapes.

Just now I spoke with two priests who, a few days ago, spoke with Mgr Kabongo, one of Pope John Paul II's two personal secretaries. Mgr Kabongo views the Medjugorje apparitions quite favourably. More importantly, he says that the Pope himself holds a very positive attitude toward the apparitions and their authenticity.

I have heard this before. Not only that the Pope and those around him look with considerable favour at Medjugorje. Also, that the head of the Sacred Congregation for the Doctrine of the Faith, Cardinal Ratzinger, sees Medjugorje in a positive way. A well-known fact: Hans Urs von Balthasar, the great Swiss theologian, and probably the greatest living Catholic theologian, stands in favour of the authenticity of the Medjugorje events with strong enthusiasm. Von Balthasar was the director of Cardinal Ratzinger's doctoral thesis, his guide and mentor; they remain close. Moreover, Father von Balthasar is the Pope's favourite theologian.

What does all this mean practically? In my opinion, these signs point to the clear possibility of a relatively early approval of the Medjugorje apparitions as authentic. This approval could come from an investigating commission of Cardinal Ratzinger's Congregation for the Doctrine of the Faith. And, I think, within four or five years. That would make Medjugorje as important as, or more important than, the shrines at Fatima and at Lourdes. Then what? Such an important Catholic shrine in a communist country could result in — what? Why let my speculation run wild? The Lord has a plan, as Jozo Zovko says. We want to recognise that plan as it unfolds, and stay obedient in faith to the Lord.

This morning, before lunch, I went to Stefanija's house and asked her to teach me Croatian for an hour a day. She said she will, insofar as she can, and refused any payment. A pretty girl, 17 years old. She has studied to be a beautician, but so far she hasn't worked anywhere. There are no beauty shops in Medjugorje. There's very little of anything — three general stores and a hardware store are all I've seen. Of course there are a couple of restaurants since Our Lady came, and the tourist bureau. No place for a beautician.

The hour lesson went well. Informal. We used mostly a book I brought from the US, written for Americans who want to learn Croatian. Stefanija is a natural teacher, patient, precise, clear, encouraging, and expecting the best from me. I may actually learn some Croatian. We meet again tomorrow at one o'clock.

This evening after Our Lady came to Jakov, Marija, and Ivan in the Franciscan house (Vicka, sick, had her visit from Our Lady at home at the same time), all three came to the sacristy just before Mass to help the priests vest. There were even more priests than Friday. And tomorrow, Sunday, there will be still more. Many groups come for the weekend, and some only for Sunday.

Jakov did not remember me, but Ivan did immediately and was quite friendly. Both he and Marija gave me special attention, spending a few concerned minutes trying to get my vestments on me in presentable shape. Always a problem. Liturgical vestments never look right on me; they hang wrong and bunch up in the wrong places. Ivan showed no surprise that I greeted him in Croatian and even spoke a few more words conversationally. The fruit of Stefanija's teaching this morning.

October 13, Sunday. Vlado Mikulic is a *guslar* here at Medjugorje, a balladeer who composes ballads and sings them on a one-stringed instrument called a *gusla*. A *gusla* looks like a little hand-carved wooden mandolin; the *guslar* plays it with a small bow, like a violin. At breakfast now with Father Philip Pavich, I'm listening to a tape of Vlado singing to his own accompaniment on the *gusla*. He sings a ballad: 'Gospi u Medjugorje', 'To Our Lady at Medjugorje'. Beautiful. It doesn't sound like anything I've ever heard. Maybe a little like Arabian singing.

Father Philip's parents were born in Croatia. He grew up in a typical American neighbourhood in Waterloo, Iowa, and joined the Sacred Heart province of the American Franciscans. Later in life he rediscovered his Croatian roots, learned the language he had heard spoken at home, and has fallen in love with Medjugorje. He leaves tonight, with me, for Dubrovnik, where we will sleep at the Franciscan house before catching the plane out on Monday. I'm sure he will come back here as soon as he can for as long a time as possible.

Philip preached at the 9.30 am English-language Mass. The church was nearly full of people, mostly a large Irish group that arrived yesterday. He said about Medjugorje: 'The simplicity of this place hits you in the face.' And he described the village, with its sheep in the narrow streets, its mud and stone huts, its down-to-earth people, as rushing into the eighteenth century. Medjugorje, Philip said, has the simplicity of the word of God. It stops the impure of heart; they can't understand it. Medjugorje has the simplicity of the Incarnation.

And it is to this simple village that Mary has come. To a village like Nazareth.

I think I understand now why the Franciscans who preach at the Masses speak so powerfully. Even when I understand nothing of what they say — almost always — I feel myself impressed and even moved by the way they say it. They speak, somehow, with power. Not loudly and not with so many gestures. But powerfully. I felt that same power this afternoon when I spoke for 45 minutes to the Italian pilgrims.

Slavko had asked me this morning to take his place at four o'clock this afternoon for a talk in Italian that he usually gives. The church was full, with many standing in the aisles. I talked about my own experiences at Medjugorje, inserting the essential information about the facts of Medjugorje. But I tried to keep it in terms of my own experience. I could feel that I was speaking strongly. My Italian, never eloquent, was eloquent. I used words and expressions I had never used before. It must have been grace, gift, because I simply cannot speak as well as I spoke this afternoon. If I didn't believe in Medjugorje, I would believe now. Thank you, Lord.

Tonight after Mass, Philip and I go to Dubrovnik, and tomorrow to Rome. I'll speak there, one talk for each of three days, on personal prayer, to the delegates from all over the world to the International Charismatic Youth Conference. Then, Friday, I'll leave Rome for Medjugorje.

I greeted Jakov and Ivanka after Mass. Ivanka looks beautiful, radiant, and immensely happy. She was walking home with some other girls, arms hooked together, laughing. I was so happy to see her.

Best of all, as if by accident, I met my old and dear friend Sister Josipa Kordic. She had just arrived with some other Franciscan sisters and priests from their house about 30 miles away. We went into the parish house and talked in the kitchen. Sister Janja came in; we went into a three-language conversation (English, Italian, Croatian) and continued until Janja threw us out so she could work. Josipa and I kept talking outside. When I return in December we'll get together again, at least during the Christmas vacation.

I'm writing this late at night in the Franciscan monastery in the old city of Dubrovnik, where Philip and I are spending the night.

It was hard to leave Medjugorje.

October 14, Monday. At the thirteenth-century Franciscan monastery in Dubrovnik's old city. At breakfast I spoke, in French, with an older priest. Like many of the older Franciscans, he has serious reservations about Medjugorje, and has never gone there. He appears to be afraid to find out that it's all true, and fearful that if he goes he might believe. I understand him.

The priest tells me that on Thursday Yugoslavian national television will present a programme, their first, on Medjugorje. About time. Germany and Italy have already had television programmes, and the London *Times* ran Medjugorje as a cover story of their Sunday supplement just eight days ago. The Yugoslavian programme will present various people expressing their views: politicians, theologians and others. Will the Yugoslavian authorities allow any fairness in the presentation? We'll see.

On board Yugoslav Airlines 406, Phil and I meet Slavko Barbaric and his provincial superior, Father Jozo Pejic, who is not an elected superior but one specially appointed, delegated, by the Minister General in Rome, John Vaughn, an American. Father Vaughn won't let the Hercegovina province elect its own superior. It's too difficult and, some say, rebellious, a province.

Before take-off for Rome. I just went up and buckled myself into the vacant seat beside Slavko (and his provincial). Slavko told me that he is going to London tomorrow to appear live on BBC television as part of a programme on Medjugorje. Next week Slavko goes to Ireland for a Medjugorje seminar. I was invited a few months ago and declined. If I had known Slavko would be there, I would have accepted.

Why all the secrecy? Slavko knew Phil and I would be on this flight. Why didn't he tell us he would be? The Franciscans at Medjugorje never give out information they don't have to. There are so many communist spies ready to trip them up. So many government agents ready to appropriate their passports. And so many secret police ready to have them put in prison. They have learned a certain affable wariness. They give nothing away.

Slavko said to me: 'It is beginning.' He meant that invitations to go abroad to speak on Medjugorje are beginning to come in. Slavko will have several, I'm sure.

★ ★ ★

October 21-27, 1985 (Lucy Rooney)

The plane from Rome to Dubrovnik arrived, as always, late — but only by one and a half hours. Father Bob Faricy and I looked around for other possible pilgrims, but saw only tourists being met by hotel buses. In the end we had to decide to take the airport bus into the town and stay the night there. Since there were only the two of us, the bus company put on a minibus for us, at a fraction of the price the taxi drivers asked.

We found rooms at the Petka — a B-class hotel, but clean and adequate, and, best of all, overlooking the Adriatic sea, just where the yachts and ferries berth. It was evening by now, and the lights of the boats sparkled on the ripples of the dark water. We walked along the sea front to check our bus for early the next morning, from the bus station. We passed the fruit and vegetable market, deserted and lamp-lit. The strings of onions, sacks of potatoes and piles of apples were there on the stalls, unguarded, mostly not even covered over. There was even a basket-work stall with all the goods displayed. There must be no thieves or vandals in Dubrovnik — no rats either?

The bus ride from Dubrovnik takes more than five hours, not because it is so far but because the road winds through the river valley between the mountains, and the bus calls at the villages and small towns en route. Every now and then everyone gets off and goes into a village bar for coffee, served Turkish-style from tiny long-handled brass pots into miniature bowls already full of sugar. Many traces of the Turkish occupation remain: the shoes with turned-up toes, the minarets.

After four and a half hours Father Bob and I abandoned the bus at Caplina and finished the journey quickly by taxi, arriving at Medjugorje just in time to be hospitably welcomed to lunch by the Franciscan priests and sisters. We found the two car parks jammed with coaches from Germany, Italy, France and Slovenia — more pilgrims than ever.

Father Tomislav Pervan arranged for us to stay with his friend Simon. Simon, tall, blond and powerfully built, worked for some years in Germany. He speaks fluent German. He and his wife Sdenka are building a new home across the farmyard from the old family house. Already they are living on the ground floor with their children Ilko, Kata and Marija. Ilko made off as soon as he knew we were arriving, but seven-year-old Kata and five-year-old Marija, despite their shyness, were so fascinated by people who could not speak Croatian that they set to work to teach us the names of things. The children, especially the girls, are so pretty, yet the women are prematurely aged. One wonders if the young generation will be different. Labour-saving washing-machines and so on are quite common, but the wind and the weather and the field work still take their toll.

In the warm kitchen heated by a wood-burning stove, we met the grandmother and the great grandmother who still live in the old house. They wear the head-kerchiefs and wide skirts of the area. The married women who are younger seem to have left off the kerchief and wear ordinary clothes, while the young are part of the denim-jean culture.

The family had given us two rooms in the unfinished upper part of the house. They were carpeted and partly furnished, but cold. However, the beds had big duvets, so it took a few minutes each early morning to decide to brave the cold room and the cold out-doors, because the bathroom was in the old house across the farmyard. Does one combine dressing gown with umbrella? Father Bob opted for overcoat, hat and scarf. There was a hot-water tank, so the first one out switched it on.

On the first evening when we went back to the church for the evening rosaries and Mass, we found the church full to the door. I managed to squeeze in out of the wind, but realised I couldn't stand for three hours, so came out and went behind the sanctuary to try — in vain — to avoid that north wind from the mountains. To get a seat, even at the back, one has to be there an hour before time. The parishioners, coming from work, cannot come early, so each evening it is they who stand at the back or outside in the bitter cold. Loudspeakers relay the Mass, and Holy Communion is brought out. Along the field beside the nave, confessions were being heard. I saw Father Tomislav Vlasic, looking like Savonarola, with his cowl pulled up over his head. After three and a half hours, I went back into the church, just as most people were leaving. At that moment the lights fused. Most of the families had brought torches to help their walk home. It was by now nine-thirty. We returned to our house for the evening meal.

One day the family killed a white hen for dinner, another day a sheep. I saw the grandmother carrying its head in a big dish, but I didn't enquire further! Each day they baked fresh bread and made sheep cheese and new butter. The older women pasture the sheep and the family cow along the verges of the roads, spinning wool or knitting as they go, or saying the rosary. One does not see so many older men. (I later discovered that many of the men were shot in the inter-Slav persecutions after the Second World War.) The women gather wood for the stoves, binding it into bundles and carrying it home on their backs. October was the time for the tobacco harvest. The plants were stripped of their leaves in the fields, the stalks left standing, then later ploughed under. When I returned to the house one day I found the mother, Sdenka, the two grandmothers, and the two great grandmothers sitting in the big shed. They sat on the floor, their legs stretched out before them, and the little black cat was charmed to be part of the group — cats are out-door animals, half wild, half wanting to be pets. The women were threading the tobacco leaves onto long strings, using large bodkins. That evening they moved the operation into the house, spreading a tarpaulin over the carpet. Next day Simon and Sdenka hauled the skeins of leaves up into the loft where they will dry out. The women's hands are permanently died black with the tobacco juice.

Most days during our stay I climbed up to the cross on Mount Krizevac. It took me 35 minutes to walk to the mountain, and 30 minutes steady going to climb up. Many old, even crippled, people make the climb. I saw several of them fall. One day a group of young people were making the stations of the cross as they went up. One of the boys carried a heavy stone on his shoulder.

Once up there, some of the pilgrims forgot their devotion, and having done their penance became festive, taking photos, smoking, and picnicking. But then, the early Christians did just that when they went to the cemeteries outside the walls of Rome, visited the graves of their dead, had Mass, then picnicked in the grassy hollows (the catacombs). It must be an instinctive part of pilgrimage!

All morning there were Masses at the church in different languages. During one English-language Mass, a group of Slovenians arrived in national dress. One sees where the habits worn by women religious originated — the pleated skirts, the short veils or coifs, the dark colours. This group came the entire length of the aisle on their knees. The only who who enjoyed it was a little three-year-old boy in long pants who scooted along on his knees with obvious glee, despite his efforts to be demure and devout.

Several evenings I abandoned the church and the weather and went into the sacristy — really so that I could talk with Marija. Marija always remembers me, and now that she speaks Italian — better than I do — we can talk. Vicka is too sick to come to church.

• *Marija receives a message from Our Lady.*

• *Vicka — vivacious but often in pain.*

Ivan was there, looking quite different, calm and more serene. Jakov arrived like a young earthquake. In the sacristy I met most of the people I wanted to see again: Father Jozo Zovko, the former pastor who had been in prison, the two young Franciscans whom the bishop had expelled, and of course Fathers Svet and Tomislav Vlasic.

★ ★ ★

October 21-27, 1985 (Robert Faricy)

October 21, Monday. Sister Lucy and I arrived here in Medjugorje last Saturday, after flying from Rome to Dubrovnik Friday afternoon. Sunday the weather turned cold and drizzly. The weekend crush of pilgrims has passed now.

So many Croatians at the Sunday Masses! Thousands. They look like country people, but they cannot be local; there just are not that many people living in this area. They come long distances, most of them by regular buses and on foot, to attend Mass at Medjugorje.

One hour of Croatian with Stefanija Saturday and another on Sunday. We'll do an hour every day.

Stefanija might go to the university in Sarajevo next year, after she finishes high school. I asked her if she'd like to go to a university in the United States. Definitely not. She wants to stay 'with Our Lady'. Stefanija looks to me like a typical high school senior, prettier than most and more intelligent. Looking at her, you might think she was American or German or Italian or anything. Young people all dress alike. But Stefanija is a high school senior from Medjugorje, and that makes all the difference. Normal in every way. She seems to have no vocation to the convent. But she loves the Blessed Virgin, and she doesn't want to leave Medjugorje for a long period of time, because Our Lady has come here, chosen this parish as her own. Apparently all or at least most of the young people here think the same way.

At high school, Stefanija studies English, German, Croatian literature, and Marxist ethics. She likes it all except for Marxist ethics. She dislikes that intensely. And, again, it seems that all the students detest Marxist studies, Marxism in general, Yugoslavian communism in particular. I tried to suggest that some of it must be good, that she could learn from it, that she can take the good parts and discard what seems false. No. She hates it.

Marxism deliberately rejects God, Jesus, Our Lady, and the Church. All that is part of Stefanija, her culture, herself, who she is. Marxism tells her that not only what she believes but also what she is, who she is, is false, wrong, a grave mistake. So behind Stefanija's rejection of Marxism and communism lies deep emotional force, a force springing from her human instinct for self-preservation, the force of Stefanija's own personal identity.

Multiply Stefanija, and you can see why Medjugorje and Our Lady here worry the local communists. Our Lady preaches ideological subversion, undermines the Marxist foundations of communism. And she appeals to the whole broad Roman Catholic tradition of the Croatian people. She's winning.

Here is Mary's message to the parish, spoken to Marija last Thursday when I was in Rome:

October 17: Dear children! Everything has its time. Today I invite you to begin working on your hearts. All the work in the fields is finished. You found the time to clean out the most abandoned places, but you have neglected your hearts. Work hard and clean up every part of your heart with love. Thank you for responding to my message.

Our Lady's messages to the parish provide the theme for the preaching at the daily Masses, and they furnish points to ponder in the hearts of all the parishioners. Mary is forming the parish spiritually.

Also last Thursday evening, the central government television station in Belgrade produced a two-hour documentary on Medjugorje. I've asked people here what they thought of the programme. In general they liked it. In particular, people here liked a long filmed interview with Ivan and Marija. And they feel that the round table or panel discussion that concluded the documentary was not so good. In fact, poor. Father Mato Kovic, a diocesan priest from Sarajevo and an important member of the commission to investigate Medjugorje, represented the Catholic side of the discussion. He took a strong stand against Medjugorje.

Television, in any language, has a way of exposing falsity and truth for what they are, as they are, no matter how the proponents of the true and the false handle themselves. It looks like that happened here. In spite of the communist government's clear intentions to debunk the Medjugorje apparitions, the truth somehow broke through and spoke to the viewers.

October 24, Thursday. Yesterday afternoon I spoke to the Italian pilgrims, almost a church-full, giving them basic information about Medjugorje. This morning I took the 9am English-language information session.

I met the American pilgrimage, just arrived, led by Sister Isabel Bettwy, went to their Mass, and spoke to them in the church after Mass and in their bus on the way to Podbrdo hill. We stopped at Marija's house. Many Italians stood at the door talking with her. She and I got on Sister Isabel's bus, and Marija answered questions through me; I acted as interpreter — she and I spoke Italian, and I translated into English for the Americans. She was beautiful. Afterward, Marija laid hands on those who were sick, praying for them. While she prayed over the sick, the rest of us said *Hail Marys*, and I led a prayer, which the others repeated after me, for the graces of conversion, of a deeper faith, and of prayer. I noticed that the group guide, a young communist who knows English, appointed to the group by the local tourist board, repeated the words of my prayer along with the others. He was quite impressed by Marija; maybe she converted him.

Tonight, at 5.50 pm, I met Father Ivan, Father Tomislav Pervan, and Serge (a young Frenchman) in the sacristy. We translated Our Lady's Thursday message to the parish, given to Marija at 5.45, into French, English, and Italian, to be read out after the Mass:

Dear children, I want to dress you from day to day in holiness, goodness, obedience, and the love of God, so that from day to day you can be more beautiful and better prepared for your Lord. Dear children, listen to my messages and live them. I desire to lead you! Thank you for responding to my call.

October 26, Saturday night. I have been really quite busy. There are a *lot* of English-speaking (especially Irish and American), French-speaking, and Italian pilgrims. They have questions and spiritual needs of all kinds. I've given several talks and homilies in English and Italian to those language groups. For the last three evenings I've either helped to lead the hour of prayer before Mass, or the time after Mass. I haven't had time for my regular hour of Croatian with Stefanija.

I take all my meals now, as I will when I return from Japan on December 2, at the house of the priests and the sisters, with them. The food is great. Especially Sister Janja's *sarma*, ground meat and rice wrapped in cabbage leaves.

Yesterday Mirjana had a visit from Our Lady. It lasted eight minutes. A month ago Mirjana heard Our Lady's voice tell her that she would come on October 25. So Mirjana knew ahead of time. She told Father Pero, and he was there during the vision. He says that, at one point, Mirjana's eyes filled with tears. Afterwards she told him that Our Lady had showed her, as in a film, the coming fulfilment of the first of the 10 secrets. It will be a severe warning to the world. She already knows the date. She'll tell Pero 10 days before it happens; and he'll make some kind of public announcement three days before it happens.

Tomislav Vlasic says that Our Lady is showing Vicka and Jakov the future of the Church and of the world. Apparently things look bad.

October 27, Sunday. Father Rastrelli, SJ, of Naples, tells me about new apparitions in Italy. He says over one hundred people at

Oliveto Citra, near Salerno, see Our Lady regularly,[1] and suggests that seven or eight of the hundred perhaps really do see her. And in Belluno, near Venice, a 14-year-old girl, Francesca, sees and speaks with Our Lady at 4.30 every afternoon. This began in early August shortly after Francesca's mother visited Medjugorje.

According to Rastrelli, whom I do trust — a good man in every way — Francesca asked Our Lady if she visited anyone at Medjugorje as she visits her. Our Lady named Jelena Vasilj, spoke some Croatian to show how she speaks to Jelena, and taught Francesca a few words in Croatian: *Gospa,* and *Majka.* Rastrelli thinks I should go to Belluno to talk to Francesca.

Serge got me the full text of Slavko's study of Jelena and Marijana. It looks really good. Sister Lucy is reading it now.

9am. Ivan, celebrating the parish 8.30 Mass, gives a long powerful sermon and, after it, baptises three babies. The parents, godparents and babies stay in the sanctuary for the whole Mass. A beautiful baptismal ceremony. Sometimes I forget that this is a parish that demands a lot of ministry from the priests and sisters. They work hard. Yet they appear always at peace, cheerful, taking time for anyone who stops them to ask advice or information.

October 28, Monday, in the Dubrovnik Airport. Sister Lucy and I left Medjugorje at 3.45 this morning in Jozo Vasilj's car, together with Margaret Leonard and Passionist Father John Mary Griffin, both from Scotland. Margaret and Father John have an early plane to Zagreb; they change there for London and Glasgow.

Last night in the sacristy, Father Tomislav Pervan suggested that, when I'm made 'emeritus professor' at the Gregorian University, I come to Medjugorje to live. He was serious. Maybe I will. Maybe even before I'm emeritus. I'd like to go back right now and stay there. Illogically enough. Medjugorje has no library. I can't work there. I can only barely speak Croatian. I find the fall and winter weather hard on my health. And Croatian peasant conditions

---

1. R Faricy, *Maria in mezzo a noi: Le apparizioni a Oliveto Citra* (Padova: Edizioni Messaggero, 1986).

of living do not suit my taste. But Our Lady is there in a special way. I'm happy there.

I will spend November in Japan, giving retreats and talks. Then, back to Medjugorje.

• Fr Robert Faricy — happy to be in Medjugorje.

3. The people at Medjugorje (December, 1985)

by Robert Faricy

December 2, Monday. After giving a weekend seminar in Ljubljana, the capital of Slovenia in northern Yugoslavia, I took the crowded night train to Split. From Split I took the Mostar bus to the Medjugorje crossroads and walked from there. I'm staying with the Kozina family: Jokan Kozina and his wife Draga, their son Marinko and his wife Sdenka, and Marinko's and Sdenka's two small children Josip and Ivana.

Sister Janja told me tonight that she hopes I can be here when Pero gets from Mirjana the secret to be revealed to the world, the prediction of some kind of imminent catastrophe that apparently will take many lives. Mirjana had another vision of it last Friday, seeing the disaster as one might see it in a film. She is badly shaken. Both Pero and Janja seem to think the fulfilment of the revelation given to Mirjana will come quite soon, at most in a few months. Pero looks nervous about his role in the matter: to know about it 10 days before it happens and to announce it three days before.

At 5 pm several of us — Slavko, Tomislav Pervan, Janja, Ignacija, and three other people — prayed in Slavko's and Ivan's office (the apparitions room). Marija and Ivan came, and we began the rosary.

Jakov on some nights has classes in his secondary school and cannot come. Our Lady comes to him when he gets home later after school, about 8 pm.

The rosary took a while. We said the joyful mysteries. Sister Janja prayerfully introduced each mystery. Then one of us led a decade of the rosary, we sang a brief hymn, led by Marija, and went on to the next mystery. I said the third mystery, leading in English; they responded in Croatian. Afterward, Marija read half of Psalm 139, slowly, pausing for short hymns every few verses. About 5.35, Ivan and Marija stood (we were all kneeling or sitting), faced the wall where Our Lady appears, and began to pray aloud, saying *Our Fathers, Hail Marys*, and *Glory be's*. Suddenly they went down on their knees. The apparition lasted about 10 minutes.

The church was not completely filled for the rosary and Mass. And relatively few people, not more than 200, stayed for the rosary after Mass. Many people worked tonight; it's hog-butchering time this week in Medjugorje.

December 3, Tuesday. My room in the Kozina house is so cold my teeth hurt. The family lives in two rooms, one for visiting and eating and one for sleeping. Both are heated. All the families I have seen here live in two rooms during the cold part of the year. Heating the whole house would cost too much. So I went to Citluk this morning with Father Pero to buy an electric heater. About 24 dollars.

'Our Lady's prayer group' met Our Lady, as they do every Monday, Wednesday, and Friday night, on one of the hills. Part of her message was the need to prepare ourselves for the feast of the Immaculate Conception, December 8, by going to confession. So I'd better go.

I'm sitting now in a confessional in the church. It's 5.45 pm. Our Lady is appearing to Jakov, Ivan, and Marija in the rectory. The church is silent. There are relatively few people. Maybe 250. There are very few pilgrims coming these days; there do not seem to be more than 50 right now.

About an hour ago I went to the rectory kitchen for a cup of tea. Marija was there helping Sister Janja prepare supper. She wants to be a sister. She'll certainly be a good one. She's a great sister already, even before she enters.

Tonight after Mass, Marija and I had a long conversation in the sacristy. We spoke in Italian. Marija's Italian has gone from good to excellent, quite fluent.

December 4, Wednesday. Today I began again my lessons with Stefanija. I am, in fact, making some progress. Stefanija's little sister Ljerka sometimes sits with us for a few minutes. Often her father joins in and teaches me. Sometimes her mother. So I have become a family project. But the best teacher by far, and the most patient, is Stefanija.

Coming back from Stefanija's house I met Marija on her way to the rectory to say the rosary with Ivan and Jakov. This time, Marija and I spoke in Croatian. She seems happy when I speak Croatian; she wants to encourage me. No one, I am convinced, could clearly manifest as much holiness as Marija, especially at such a young age, unless that person were somehow directly guided by Jesus or Mary. Holiness is shown in love, and Marija is extraordinarily loving.

I asked Marija how Our Lady speaks Croatian, with what kind of accent. Marija answered that she speaks exactly like the people here in Medjugorje, with just the same accent. I find myself quite moved by that fact.

To think that Mary so completely adapts herself to the young people to whom she appears and speaks. In different ways, she does the same thing for each of us. Our Lady comes to each of us on our own terms so to speak, in terms of who we are, our background and culture, our problems. She acts as a real mother for each one individually, personally. This comes across strongly in her daily appearances to the young people. But it holds just as true for me and for you.

Lord Jesus, help me to take your mother and her love for me seriously. Thank you for giving me your own mother as my heavenly mother. Thank you for sending her to help me, to mother me, to pray with me and for me. Thank you for her love. Help me to respond to her love by taking her hand and letting her lead me to you and unite me more closely with you. Amen.

Marija and I arrived at the rectory after a short walk. She went in to say the rosary and to wait for Our Lady, who will come about 5.40 or 5.45; and I came here to sit in the confessional and to wait for people who want to go to confession in a language I can speak. A sign on the confessional says, 'English, Italiano, Français'. So far I've had a few confessions in Italian. And I've had some free time to write these lines.

December 5, Thursday. Our Lady gave this message for the parish to

Marija tonight at 5.45 pm in the rectory:

Dear children! I call you to prepare yourselves for Christmas by penance, prayer, and works of charity. Do not look at the material, because then you will not be able to experience Christmas.

December 6, Friday. I spoke with Slavko this morning. And I asked to be in the rectory room this evening when Our Lady appears. So I'll go there a little before 5 pm.

Sister Josipa Mara Kordic visited yesterday; it was good to see her. We walked to the post office together and telephoned Sister Lucy Rooney to say Hello. It cost only four dollars to telephone to Rome on a weekday afternoon.

Philip Pavich is here for a few days. His Croatian is good, and he helped me today with mine, which remains really bad.

December 7, Saturday. Because December 8 falls on Sunday, the Church celebrates the feast of the Immaculate Conception today. The number of people at evening Mass has grown during the week. Last night all the seats were filled, and many people were standing. The church will be packed tonight.

At meals the Franciscan priests and sisters have great conversations with much laughter. Ivan and Slavko are both wonderful story-tellers. I understand maybe three per cent of the conversation. Often, after the meal, the fathers, who have been at one half of the table, leave; and the sisters stay for their own little conversation.

During the meal the sisters listen mostly and laugh at the witty things the fathers say. Except Sister Janja, who more than holds her own. The other three sisters are all naturally quiet people. Janja is lively, cheerful, articulate. She speaks good English, and she's learning Italian.

December 8, the Second Sunday of Advent. All last week you could see the hogs and sheep being killed and butchered in the back yards of the houses along the road to where I live in the Kozina house. But today is quiet in the village. This morning the church is filled for the 8.30 Mass in Croatian. At 9.30 Philip Pavich and I will say the Mass in English in the little side chapel where Our Lady used to appear before the bishop ordered her out, while the German-language Mass will take place in the main nave of the church.

Pilgrims, especially Italians and Swiss and Austrians, are beginning to arrive in their buses. By 5 this afternoon they will fill the church and spill out into the area in front of it. And over one hundred will stand silently outside the window of the rectory room where Our Lady will appear between 5.30 and 6 this evening.

Make ready the way of the Lord, the Gospel says today. The word 'way' in both English and the original Greek is the same word used in the Acts of the Apostles to describe Christianity: it's the 'Way'. Paul uses the same word in I Corinthians, chapters 12 and 13: 'I will show you a still more excellent *way*.' A way more excellent than the gifts and charisms he's talked about in chapter 12, a way that includes all the gifts and charisms and without which they are nothing at all. The way is love. Christianity is about love. The way of the Lord is the way of love. Make straight the way of the Lord.

And this happens to us here at Medjugorje. Jesus through Mary makes straight the way of love, straightens out the love, all the loves, in our lives, teaches us to love.

To love with an open hand, not possessively. To love freely, leaving the other person free. Not grasping or hanging on, not using the one I love like an object; loving as Jesus loves us, straight — the way of the Lord.

Mary takes me on the way of the Lord, the way of love, to Jesus. Medjugorje means precisely that. Mary takes my hand and leads me to Jesus along his way of love.

Paul prays in today's second reading that my love may abound in understanding and in experience. In understanding: that I might know Jesus through love, understand him through love. And know, understand, other people through love.

In experience: that I may experience the Lord's love for me and also my love for him. That I may grow in the experience of loving the Lord and other people, and of receiving love from the Lord and from others.

Holiness is the infinite capacity to love and to receive love. Only God is truly holy. But I can grow in holiness. I can, here and now in this holy place, grow in the capacity to receive the Lord's love and to love him back, grow in the capacity to love others and to receive their love.

Mary, Mother of Divine Love, pray for us. Pray for me.

Also here: Eleanor McFadden of the Dublin Medjugorje Centre, in hurricane force as always, full of complete trust in the power of the Lord. Seeing her builds me up.

December 10, Tuesday. I spoke for about 40 minutes this morning with Father Anto Bakovic from the Sarajevo archdiocese. He came for a brief visit. Father Anto holds the record for a Yugoslavian priest doing time in prison: four times. The second time he did six years that included the period of the Second Vatican Council. He didn't know anything about the Council, only that it was going on. And he offered every day of his suffering for the Council, for Church renewal, and for priests.

Anto Bakovic, once out of prison, built a whole parish plant, seven large buildings, with no outside funding. In fact, he was accused of embezzlement by Church authorities who couldn't figure out how he did it.

He's a tough man, 54 years old, with a 'lean and hungry look' like Shakespeare's Cassius. He looks like 40. Anto asked me: 'Why does the Church stink of worldly diplomacy? Why does the Vatican not name *apostles* to the Yugoslavian bishoprics instead of *diplomats*?' I have no answer for that. Father Bakovic impressed me with his meekness and his humility as well as his courage.

Last night, Monday, the Irish group from Cork and the Italians from Cosenza went up on Mount Krizevac with Ivan's little prayer group. At 11 pm Our Lady appeared to Vicka and Ivan (Marija was absent) with five angels. Vicka said through an interpreter that Our Lady welcomed each one, thanked them for coming up the mountain, laid her hands on the heads of all present, and said that she has a plan for each one — and that each should prepare spiritually for Christmas.

Up until Our Lady's appearance finished, the sky was bright with stars. As soon as she left, it clouded over completely.

Yesterday Tomislav Pervan and Sister Janja and I drove to Citluk for shopping and to get some meat ground. Meat from the recently slaughtered animals. When we were alone Sister Janja told me that Father Pervan is good to go shopping with; his heart is so big he lets her buy whatever she wants.

Today, Sister Janja made about 65 pounds of sausage out of the ground meat. We had some for supper. I've never had sausage that good.

After Mass I stayed in the sacristy with Sister Ignacija and Vicka for the prayers for healing of the sick — beautifully led by Father Tomislav Vlasic — and the glorious mysteries of the rosary. Vicka is very ill, and clearly in much physical suffering.

The weekend rush is over. Very few pilgrims remain. Only a few Italians and French, a small group from England, a group from Cork. And Dick and Joan Downing, from near Boston, with three of their children — Lisa, Bonnie, and Peter — and a grandchild, Rachel, all staying here with me in the Kozina house.

December 11, Wednesday. Evenings, at twilight, going from Stefanija's house to the church at about 5 pm or a little before, I can see a quite bright light at the base of the cross up on Mount Krizevac, like a bonfire or a searchlight. I asked Sister Janja about it yesterday. She said there's no light up there, and that probably it's one of the many signs that people see especially about five in the evening when the rosary is about to begin in the church. And she added: 'I never see any signs.' I'll have to show her the light on Krizevac.

The parish of St James in the Medjugorje area has five villages. The village of Medjugorje, the first one you come to on the road that leads off the road between the Adriatic coast and Mostar, has the post office. So the whole complex of the five villages can be referred to as Medjugorje.

I live in Medjugorje, down a side road to the right as you go towards St James's Church. So when I go to the church or the rectory, I take my little road from the Kozina house past the ancient houses that crowd right up to the roadside, turn right at the road from the highway to the church, pass the post office on my left, and cross the deplorably dilapidated and railingless bridge that the local government refuses to repair and that some day a bus will drive off and into the little river that runs past the church. The road over the bridge turns right to the church and rectory grounds, and then left again to go past them to the village of Bijakovici where Stefanija lives and where, well beyond her house and to the right, the four young people who see Our Lady live. Their homes are close together in the main and most densely built part of Bijakovici, where the centuries-old stone houses line the road with little or no spaces between them. This section of Bijakovici is called 'Podbrdo'. The name means 'the foot of the hill'. Here on June 24, 1981, Mirjana and Ivanka first saw Our Lady up on the hillside as they walked along a gravel road near the bottom of the hill, a little way from the houses. On the following days, the two 16-year-old girls, together with the four who now continue to see and speak with Mary daily, met with Our Lady on that same hillside now marked with a well-worn path and several wooden crosses hand-made by pilgrims.

Beyond the hill lies the village of Surmanci. Vionica, where Sister Josipa was born and where her family lives, stands between Bijakovici and the highway to Mostar. The fifth village, Miletina, is to the right of Medjugorje as you go toward the church. Looking down into the valley from where the cross tops Mount Krizevac, on a good day you can locate the five villages in the flat plain ringed by rocky hills.

December 12, Thursday. Here is the message given by Our Lady to Marija this evening for the parish:

> *Dear children! For Christmas I invite you to give glory to Jesus together with me. I will give him to you in a special way on that day, and I invite you on that day to give glory and praise with me to Jesus at his birth. Dear Children, pray more on that day, and think more about Jesus. Thank you for responding to my call.*

I did the 'official' translation into English from the Croatian. I know just barely enough Croatian to do that, and I feel it's a great privilege to do it.

December 13, Friday. Tomislav Vlasic stopped by the rectory last night after supper on his way to his parish in Vitina, near Ljibuski, after a meeting with Bishop Zanic in Mostar. The bishop had called for him. Tomislav told me not to write anything about the meeting.

When I was in Japan in November the bishop called in the parish staff and spoke to them. Sister Janja talked to me about that meeting a little bit this morning. Apparently it was pretty bad.

From speaking with Bishop Zanic and from reading what he has written and made public, I know that: (1) he has completely and irrevocably convinced himself that the Marian apparitions here are a total hoax put up by the Franciscans; and (2) that Father Tomislav Vlasic has masterminded the whole enterprise and continues to oversee it.

I simply do not understand the bishop. A doubt, even serious doubts, I could understand. But absolute certitude of complete falsity? The kind of temerity that risks fighting God and God's mother head-on really puzzles me. Slavko and Tomislav say they understand him. I do not understand him at all.

There are only a few pilgrims now: 12 English-speaking, for whom I say Mass every morning at 10; about as many Italians; no French or German-speaking pilgrims. In the evening the church fills up with people from the parish and from this region.

So it's calm here. And, after three rainy days, sunny. The river bed, dry for months, now holds a fast-flowing and ample river that makes a quiet noise as it goes under the bridge, along the road, and past the church.

Draga Kozina walks back and forth on the flat roof by my window carrying bundles of tobacco leaves. Past her I can see the mountains in the distance and, closer, our own mountains with Mount Krizevac and its cross clear against a cloudless light blue sky. I think I like Medjugorje best like this: timeless, immobile, a place for hermits. I find it hard to realise at this moment that the people here really belong to the late twentieth century, that they have radios and cars, and that after church tonight most of them will watch their favourite television programme, *Dynasty*.

December 15, the Third Sunday of Advent. The non-Yugoslavians who live here, or who stay here much of the time, form a small and quite interesting group. One of the most interesting: Anne-Carin, a Belgian girl about 25 years old, who helps Father Slavko in various matters, especially in translating things into French. Most of her time she spends in prayer. She receives interior locutions — messages — from Our Lady. She has already in the past two weeks given me four messages from Mary. All four have helped me, especially the last one, which particularly concerns my community life back at the Gregorian University and how I should act in community. I'm sure it's really from Our Lady; neither Anne-Carin, nor anyone here, could possibly know that much about me and about my community situation.

In the late afternoons I see Anne-Carin in church before the evening services, praying alone or with a pilgrim. She sometimes prays with people for healing. During the services I see her there praying with real reverence even though she knows only a little Croatian. After Mass she goes to Slavko's room to work there with Milona, the German girl who helps Slavko especially with English.

Milona's English is excellent. She acted as interpreter for Slavko when he toured Ireland giving talks. She's teaching Slavko English. He already speaks more than well enough to make announcements in English in church. Together they read several pages of my book *Seeking Jesus in Contemplation and Discernment* every day. Slavko told me it will be the first complete book he will have read in English.

Anne-Carin and Milona are a striking pair: Anne-Carin — slender with straight black hair and dark shining eyes, pretty, leaning forward when she walks as though on some urgent mission; and Milona — over six feet, erect and handsome, with abundant long hair in a sort of German Afro hair-style; she could be the Queen of the Valkyries. She has a brilliant mind, speaks several languages quite fluently, and above all lives completely for God.

Both girls are clearly special and quite specially chosen by the Lord. I feel privileged to know them.

They were both at Jakov's house tonight for a party. We were the only people there who don't speak Croatian. A great party: Fathers Pero, Slavko, Jozo Zovko; some sisters from this area, Anne-Carin and Milona, a few people I'd never seen, and Marija and Jakov. And my friend Sister Josipa Kordic, a close friend of Jakov and especially of Marija. And of course Jakov's aunt, uncle and two small girl-cousins. Slavko led the singing and made jokes. He was terrific. Jakov loved it.

Just before the party ended, Vicka and Ivan came and greeted everyone. I never did find out what the occasion for the party was. I understood nearly nothing of the conversation.

Jakov will almost certainly enter the Franciscan order as soon as they'll take him. He may have to wait two or three years. He could, of course, enter the minor seminary in Dubrovnik right away. But I doubt that he will. It would be a tough life to live in a minor seminary when you see and speak with Our Lady every day, and when several of the priest faculty members and supervisors don't at all believe in the Medjugorje events. Ivan tried it a few years ago and it did not work out.

December 16, Monday. Archbishop Franc Franic, the Archbishop of Split and the ranking Croatian-speaking prelate in this whole region, visited Medjugorje today on the anniversary of his consecration as a bishop. He made a private visit, of course, nothing official; it is not his diocese. He said a private Mass, we had lunch, and then he went to visit Vicka at her house. He's a brilliant theologian and a holy man.

Last night and tonight I anointed Vicka with non-sacramental oil blessed for use in praying for healing. When I anointed her last night she resisted and said 'No' at first. She seems to not want to get better. I think she may be hanging on to her sickness. She's suffering for love of the Lord; she understands the meaning of her suffering, and she wants to carry her cross with Jesus.

Anyway, I intend to anoint her every day that she comes to evening Mass until she's healed or until she tells me to stop, whichever comes first. She certainly has a strong will, and she says just what she thinks. So she can just tell me to quit anointing her if she doesn't like it.

December 17, Tuesday. Sister Josipa arrived about 8.30 in the morning. We talked and prayed; I said the regular 10 o'clock Mass for English-speaking pilgrims. Then we went to visit Vicka; Goyko — Stefanija's father — stopped his taxi when he saw us, and drove us to Vicka's. And he waited for us while we were there. He wouldn't take any money.

Vicka's health seems a lot better. She is her vivacious self again. I told her, through Josipa who translated my Italian into Croatian, that I felt the Lord wanted to give her healing graces — of what kind, whether of physical or spiritual healing, or all kinds of healing, I don't know. But I told her I'd like to anoint her with oil blessed for healing once a day.

Sister Josipa and I had lunch at her mother's house. Josipa's mother is 75. In her house live her son and daughter-in-law and their five children. We all prayed for each person individually while I blessed each one in turn.

Although Josipa's mother was born well after the Turkish occupation of Hercegovina had ceased, she nevertheless has the traditional tattoos on her forearms: three or four small crosses on each arm. I've seen them on several older women here. The practice began under the Turks. Turkish soldiers would flee from the Christian cross, so the Christian women had the little tattooed crosses to avoid molestation from the soldiers. Even after the Turks left, the custom continued.

Toward the end of my daily Croatian lesson with Stefanija, a high-school teacher from Mostar dropped in to visit the family. At the time Stefanija and I were reading a passage from our textbook that puts forth a lot of propaganda about Yugoslavian communism. Stefanija, although an excellent Catholic and an intelligent girl, believes the propaganda. I asked the professor if it were true, for example, as the book says, that Yugoslavia really lives up to its professed policy of non-alignment and does not belong at all to the Soviet bloc. He answered: 'I do not really know you, so I will not answer your question.' He was afraid.

After the lesson I went to the rectory where Sister Janja dragooned me into taking charge of the apparitions room. She was busy supervising the painting of the inside of the house, and Father Slavko was not around. The apparition was several minutes long tonight.

Walking to the church for Mass afterward with Marija, I had another lesson about living in a non-free society. Marija said that two men came to see her and asked her a lot of questions. They spoke Italian and said they were Italian journalists. She thought they might be not Italian but Yugoslavian, and perhaps not journalists at all. But, unlike the professor, Marija has no fear.

Except when she has to speak or read in public. In the novena before Christmas, Marija reads a canticle, for example the canticle of Zechariah, at the end of Mass just before the last blessing. It scares her to death. This evening in the sacristy I prayed with her for a minute for the grace to read in public, explaining first that reading Scripture publicly is a gift, a charism. And I asked the Lord to take away her fear.

December 18, Wednesday. After the 10 o'clock English-language Mass, Milona took me in her car to Vicka's house to anoint her for healing. Vicka sat at a table with Jakov writing Christmas cards and addressing envelopes. I stayed only two or three minutes, just long enough to anoint her and to say a short prayer.

As I started for the church at 5 this evening, Sister Janja pushed me into the room where the apparitions take place for the rosary and the apparitions. Jakov had evening classes and will have his meeting with Our Lady at home later tonight. Vicka had her visit from Our Lady at home. But Ivan and Marija were there. Father Slavko acted as supervisor as he always does except when for some reason he can't be present.

Marija led the joyful mysteries and four decades of the sorrowful mysteries. She introduced each mystery with a few sentences in Croatian. Each of us led a decade in his or her own language.

As always, Ivan and Marija said nothing of what happened during the apparition. Most of what Our Lady says applies only to them, guidance for their own lives. Once in a while Mary will give them something for another person or persons, and in that case of course they pass on what Our Lady said. But usually it's just for themselves.

How does Mary guide these young people? No one seems to know what she tells them. For example, when asked whether or not he will study for the priesthood, Ivan says only that Our Lady has a plan for him. He says it quite serenely. Our Lady has obviously given him a great grace of hope.

The priests here do not see how Ivan can ever be a priest. He lacks the necessary educational background to enter a seminary. No seminary in Croatia or Hercegovina would take him. He lacks the personal and intellectual qualities to study abroad. So, still according to the priests here, there appears little hope for Ivan's vocation. But he seems confident and serene.

December 19, Thursday. At breakfast I asked Slavko why he didn't eat anything. We fasted yesterday, and today I'm eating like a very hungry man. Slavko tells me he's fasting on bread and water for the nine days before Christmas. He says he feels just as strong and has just as much energy as when he eats regularly. He began his fast without any planning or premeditation.

Fasting is a grace, even a charism. When we fast, we co-operate with a special grace. If I try to fast without praying for the gift of fasting, I get weak and have headaches. Slavko, obviously, has acted under the inspiration of the Holy Spirit to fast. His present fasting not only co-operates with God's grace; it manifests the power, the efficacy, of grace.

Medjugorje: a place of special graces: *'Medju gore'* — 'between the mountains'. *'Gore'* has four possible meanings according to whether the 'o' and the 'e' are long or short. For instance, *'Gore gore gore gore'* means 'Up there the mountains are burning even more'.

Up there on Podbrdo where the early apparitions took place, up there on Mount Krizevac where the big cross stands, the mountains burn every day with more grace, with that fire between Jesus and the Father, the fire that came down on the heads of Mary and the disciples in the upper room at Pentecost, the fire that burned in Mary at the first Christmas and that burns in her heart now, even more, for each of us. That fire is the Holy Spirit.

Up there in heaven and up on the hills and down here between the mountains, in this specially chosen little parish, the fires of the Spirit of Jesus, tended here by his mother, burn brightly — in Marija reading Scripture in public, in Ivan hoping in his vocation to the priesthood, in Slavko fasting, and even in me.

The fire of Jesus' Spirit burns in us and makes things easy. Marija can read now in church with less fear. Ivan hopes with serenity. Slavko says: 'I know this fast comes from the Holy Spirit because it's not difficult; if it were difficult I couldn't do it!'

And even I, with the Lord's grace, with the fire of his Spirit burning in me, even I can live in a small cold room in a Herzegovinian village, speaking the language only a little, cut off from the outside world, with no *Time* magazine, no news on television, no telephone, no car. And I do find it easy. Thank you, Lord. Thank you, Mary.

Slavko and Sister Janja were tied up this evening, so I took charge of the apparitions period in Slavko's and Ivan's bedroom-office. Nothing to do really, just be the responsible person. Marija led the joyful and sorrowful mysteries of the rosary, introducing each mystery in Croatian and indicating the person to lead the decade in his or her native language.

As always, the apparition began with Marija and Ivan falling to their knees when Mary came. It continued in silence. Marija and Ivan spoke to Mary, and of course she spoke to them, but we could hear nothing. After some minutes, as always, Marija and Ivan said one *Our Father* and one *Glory be* together with Mary for peace in the world. They never include the *Hail Mary*; Mary wouldn't be praying to herself! When Marija and Ivan pray with Mary we can hear them. After the prayer, the apparition always goes on in silence.

Since it's Thursday evening, Our Lady gave Marija a message for the parish.

Dear children! Today I want to invite you to love your neighbour. If you love your neighbour you will experience Jesus more, especially on Christmas day. God will give you great gifts if you abandon yourselves to him. I want to give to mothers in particular on Christmas day my special maternal blessing. And Jesus will bless the others with his blessing. Thank you for responding to my call.

Tomislav Vlasic's prayer group, guided by Our Lady through Jelena Vasilj and Marijana Vasilj, met tonight, so Tomislav ate supper with us. An Italian priest was present, so the three of us spoke Italian.

I asked Tomislav why, if Ivan has a priestly vocation, he doesn't start studying somewhere to prepare himself. Tomislav answered that all six young people have personal private secrets, over and beyond the nine or 10 secrets that each has regarding the world. And they have to live out the elements of those secrets. Apparent meaning: Our Lady wants Ivan here, doing what he does, ordinary manual work, for the time being.

I also asked both Tomislav and Slavko about Ivanka, now living in Mostar. Does she have anyone looking after her spiritually, the way Father Pero helps Mirjana? No, they answered, because nothing special is going on right now in her life. Tomislav spoke to her a few days ago, and she's fine.

December 20, Friday. I have been wondering precisely why I am here and what the Lord really wants me to do here. The words came quite distinctly during breakfast. 'I did not send you here to minister.' Not that I should not minister to people; I do to some extent. But this is not the Lord's real purpose in having me here.

Why am I here? So that the Lord can prepare me for whatever comes after this and in the years to come. I am here to find the Lord. And to find myself in him. I'm a pilgrim, and I'm here for the same reason that other pilgrims come to Medjugorje: to find the Lord and his will, to receive his forming and strengthening love through his mother.

The investigating commission named by the bishop, about 14 members, will not meet again until next May. They met here at the end of November for two days. Only seven or eight came. Most of those present were in the rectory room for the apparitions twice. They did not make any comments about anything. Father Ivan, who belongs to the commission, says that about half believe in the authenticity of the apparitions and half do not.

I really do not see how anyone at all prayerful can be present for an apparition and have serious doubts about its authenticity. Again tonight I was responsible for the apparitions room. Ivan led the joyful and sorrowful mysteries. It went well.

December 21, Saturday. Hardly any German or Italian-speaking pilgrims, but little groups of English speakers come and go. They usually attend our regular 10 o'clock Mass in the little chapel Our Lady used to come to. It's a holy place. Milona and Anne-Carin have started coming to the English Mass.

We do, I feel, receive real graces during that Mass, especially the grace of peace. Peace is the special grace of Medjugorje.

Slavko asked me this morning to write a prayer for peace. I don't know what he intends to do with it. Here it is:

> Mary, Mother of God,
> my mother, Queen of Peace,
> ask your Son Jesus
> to give me the gift of peace.
> Pray for me for peace:
> peace in my heart,
> peace of mind and of soul,
> peace in my family,
> peace with all whom I meet,
> the peace of Jesus.
>
> Jesus, my Lord and Saviour,
> my Brother, King of Peace,
> I come to you with Mary, Queen of Peace,
> to ask you humbly for a new outpouring
> of the gift of peace.
> Pour out on me your Holy Spirit of Peace.

Give me peace, Jesus,
peace within myself,
peace in my family,
peace in my everyday life.
Give peace to my nation, and to all nations,
peace among all peoples,
peace in the world.

Jesus, my mediator with the Father,
take me to the Father to pray for peace.

Father, Father of Jesus,
our Father, my Father,
I come to you with your Son Jesus.
In him and with him and through him
I pray for peace:
peace inside me,
peace around me,
peace in the world.

  Amen.

This afternoon I signed over to Milona all translation, publication, and royalty rights to *Seeking Jesus in Contemplation and Discernment* for the German, Dutch, and all the Yugoslavian languages. I hope she can get the book into German at least.

While she signed the document, I discovered that her full name is Milona von Habsburg. She has, certainly, all the Habsburg features that you can see in the paintings: the long face and jaw, the height, the same eyes. Not, it turns out, the mythical Queen of the Valkyries, but the real Archduchess of Austria.

Tonight, during the time of the apparition, Sister Janja and I said the rosary in the community rectory, next to the room where Mary appears. Right after Our Lady left, Marija rushed into the room looking for a piece of paper. I gave her my pen. She wrote down the message Our Lady had just given her for the young people of the parish. Our Lady addresses them not as she has always begun her messages to the parish — 'Dear children' — but '*Dragi*'. *Dragi* means something like 'loved ones' or 'dear ones'. It's used in families.

I find it interesting that Mary avoids calling them children. Here is the message.

> *Dear ones! Rejoice over all that God has done for you. You are not at all aware of what God has given you. I want to tell you to pray and to live the messages that I give you. I have great confidence in you young people.*

December 22, Sunday. I used that message and last Thursday's message for my homily at the English Mass this morning. Then we all prayed together:

— to be more aware of the graces offered us here now;
— to love our neighbour, and to experience Jesus more in our lives;
— to abandon ourselves more completely to the Lord, and to open our hearts to receive the great gifts he offers us.

Father Francis Donnelly arrived late this evening from Rome. The pilgrims are beginning to arrive for Christmas. Not so many; certainly not as many as when we have warmer weather. However, we have no French or Italian priests here. Francis will help out with the confessions in French and Italian as well as English, and he'll say the Italian Mass. As always, Francis is full of the Holy Spirit and radiates goodness and gladness. A Christmas person.

Christmas Eve, December 24, Tuesday. This morning at 6.10, as I do every morning, I left the Kozina house to walk to the church for morning prayer — matins and lauds — and Mass with the Franciscan priests and sisters. Down the road in the cold dark, past the mushroom factory on my left, Medjugorje's only real industry, where the night sentry sits immobile in his sentry box, over the dilapidated bridge to the church. It means much to me to pray and say Mass with my brothers and sisters.

I certainly get enough liturgy here. Mass early in the morning. Then, later in the morning, either the Mass for English-speaking pilgrims or the Italian Mass.

I don't concelebrate the evening Mass in Croatian at 6. Two Masses are enough to say. But I go to it, in the sacristy. I try to follow the homily.

Marija comes to the sacristy after the apparition to hear Mass. Vicka usually now comes to the evening Mass after her apparition at home. Her health looks better.

Last night Jakov was there, too, as he frequently is. He acted silly, teasing Marija during the Mass. He's only 14, but even for 14 he seems immature. He wore his scarf on his head like a turban, just to be funny, and in general cut up at Mass. I've been praying for him a lot. He and Ivan are almost exact opposites. Ivan: taciturn, even dour, sometimes brusque, serious, reserved. Jakov: animated, cheerful, mischievous, outgoing, fun-loving. They're both quite normal.

I won't go to Stefanija's for my Croatian lesson until next Monday, and then I'll stop again until after New Year's; I'll begin again on January 3. Stefanija has no Christmas vacation. School closes during the whole month of January, but even Christmas eve and Christmas day schools stay in session. It's a communist country.

Stefanija goes to high school in Mostar with Croatians, Serbs, Moslems, and atheists. She has to keep going to school right through Christmas. But as for the schools that have only Croatians, even though school stays open, no students go on Christmas eve and on Christmas day. They simply stay home, and the school officials understand. No classes.

Certainly the communist government no longer persecutes Catholics the way it did in the past for several years after the Second World War. After the war many priests, especially the Franciscans of this region, met martyrdom. A large number burned alive on February 22, 1945, in a bunker in the back yard of the convent where Sister Josipa lives. Many others were thrown off a cliff that you can see on the road to Dubrovnik.

The younger priests especially died or went to prison for several years, where they were tortured in various ways. Speaking casually with one this afternoon, I found he had spent five years in prison: 1945-1948 and 1952-1954. The prisons here are unbelievably severe, and especially severe for priests.

Sisters, too, have suffered. It amuses me when I find that American sisters think the Croatian sisters conservative because they wear the habit. In fact, not all of them do; many wear secular clothes with no identifying sign or crucifix or medal.

After the war, the government did what it could to stamp out the religious life. No sister could wear religious garb from 1945 until 1957. Even now, the older sisters do not wear the habit. The sisters under 60 or so, perhaps braver, all do. The categories 'conservative' and 'progressive' just do not apply to them. They are courageous and free.

The government, of course, still persecutes the Church. Here at Medjugorje the government harassment is almost beyond belief. The Franciscans can't even build what they absolutely need, like toilets for the pilgrims.

But they're alive, and not in prison. So things have improved over the years.

Christmas Day. More pilgrims today, over 100 Italians and about 80 or so English-speaking. Since we expected a smaller number of Italians, we scheduled the Italian and English language Masses both for noon, intending the Italian Mass to take place in the small chapel. But too many Italians came, so we had one Mass, in the church, switching the language back and forth between English and Italian. We sang hymns everyone could sing, 'Adeste Fideles', 'Regina Coeli' and 'Silent Night', with each person singing in his or her own language. A beautiful Mass, with a spirit of unity among all the language groups present: mostly Italian and English, with some German, Dutch, and French.

Tonight I had Christmas dinner at the home of Slavko's brother Jozo, with Slavko's mother, brothers, nieces (many, no nephews), and several cousins. His mother is beautiful with quite strong features — the kind of face portrait-painters like. We ate *sarma*, which I like, and chicken and many other things.

December 26, Thursday. I came to the church at 6.20 this morning for morning prayer and Mass. But the Franciscans apparently had scheduled it for later.

I sat by the side of the church and watched a strange yellow-rose dawn struggle trying to lift the dark grey cloud curtain. It fell back defeated. A John the Baptist of the sun. Failed, like the first.

The Medjugorje-Mostar bus went by at 6.22 carrying high-school students to their classes. Then only the sound of roosters crowing. And an occasional bustling noise in his sleep from Gary, the priests' dog. The top dog of canine stupidity. I could have stolen the church and not disturbed his sleep.

It began to rain, and I moved to stand in the church doorway to write this by daylight. A few flies sleep on the yellow stucco wall next to me. The Franciscans' lights are on. Talking children come down the road past the church grounds on the way to the elementary school a hundred yards beyond the rectory. One of the priests comes from the rectory and unlocks the church door. The day begins.

Here's the message Our Lady gave Marija for the parish during the apparition this evening:

> *Dear children! I want to thank all of you who have listened to my messages, and who have lived on Christmas Day what I told you. I want to guide you, purified now from your sins, from now on to go forward in love. Abandon your hearts to me. Thank you for responding to my call.*

December 27, Friday. This morning Sister Janja makes dough in the kitchen for strudel. She will make cheese strudel for the main dish at lunch, and apple strudel for dessert at supper. She spreads the dough out on the long green-topped kitchen table; it covers the whole table and hangs two feet over the sides.

Later: I said the 9.30 morning Mass in French for about 20 people in the small chapel off the sanctuary. When we finished, the English-speaking people in the nave were singing 'Silent Night'. The French and French-Canadians left the chapel and came down into the nave singing as they went. 'Silent Night' in both English and French — a beautiful symbol of the kind of international community we have here.

Back in the kitchen before lunch, I sampled the cheese strudel — delicious. And I asked Sister Janja what Mirjana and Ivanka, the two young people who already have the 10 secrets (the others have eight or nine), do now. Mirjana studies agriculture at the University of Sarajevo. Ivanka keeps house for her widowed father and her sister in Mostar. Ivanka's family has a small tobacco field and a vineyard here in Medjugorje. She comes sometimes, especially in the summer, to work in the field and the vineyard.

Sister Lucy arrives tomorrow evening. Jozo Vasilj will pick her up at the Split airport; she will stay for a week at Jozo's house.

Father Ivan has been quite ill with a fever for two days. Since he lives in the room where the apparitions take place, and since he has to stay in bed, the apparitions last night and tonight took place in the rectory basement in the hall for catechism classes and information sessions for pilgrims. Several Italian groups have come for the week between Christmas and New Year. We had a mob scene tonight outside the hall with everyone wanting to get into the apparitions room. In the end, Slavko let in only the priests and the people close to the door. I had the apparitions room tonight (Slavko took the rosary in church).

December 28, Saturday. Angela, the dynamic housewife from Bologna, has probably done more than anyone else to make Medjugorje known in northern Italy. She has organised several pilgrimages, and she makes frequent short visits here. And she keeps Italy informed by a telephone network of what happens in Medjugorje.

As I walked home tonight after a day full of ministering to people, mostly Italians, a car stopped next to me — Angela, her husband, their beautiful daughter, and Father Jozo Zovko, the pastor at the time of the first apparitions. I got into the car. They wanted to take me to dinner, but I was too tired.

Angela told me that when she arrived the other day in Split the police arrested her for espionage and smuggling, seized her passport, and released her only after a preliminary trial. Tomorrow she returns to Split for more time in court. The absurd charges will not, of course, hold up. But we never know what the police will do.

December 29, Sunday. I continue to anoint Vicka for healing every evening at some point during the Mass. She likes it, and seems to look forward to it.

Sister Lucy has come. And this evening, during the regular late supper, Father René Laurentin walked into the dining room. He had driven down from Brussels with some friends. They've gone to the chapel for Mass, and they'll have their supper later. René Laurentin has not come to Medjugorje for a year. The Yugoslav government banned him for one year last Christmas, for bringing into the country a few books in French. He has, nevertheless, kept up his intensive research on the events here, by letter and through emissaries. Now he can do it first-hand. It's good to see him again.

Father Ivan B, who has visited here several times over the Christmas holidays, a Franciscan of the Herzegovina province who works in America, has gone to Mostar, called there by the police. They will question him — not about anything in particular, but as the usual form of harassment and intimidation. The community here prays for him especially today.

December 30, Monday. René Laurentin brought with him a video camera and a man to run it. They made a videotape of the apparition this evening. Father Laurentin's energy and drive do not conflict at all with his essential kindness and gentleness. He will stay only a few days, and then return to France.

December 31, Tuesday. As we finished breakfast, Father Laurentin came in and sat down at the table. We talked for about 30 minutes. René Laurentin asks good questions quickly — a great information getter. He wants all the facts, and he takes ample notes. I profited from the conversation, which concerned the diocesan commission. It has 13 regular members, not including the bishop, who, though not really a member, exercises great influence by his presence at the meetings. Three doctors also belong to the commission: two from Zagreb and one from Citluk.

Five members out of the total of 16 stand strongly opposed to Medjugorje. All the members without exception recognise the great spiritual fruits here. But the five opposed maintain that these fruits are simply normal Croatian piety.

Last night Ivan and Marija passed the word that their small prayer group would meet Our Lady on Podbrdo at 10.30 pm. About 150 people showed up to pray and sing until Mary came. The apparition lasted about 10 minutes. Our Lady asked for prayers for the suffering and the starving.

The small group used to meet Our Lady, who appears to Ivan and to Marija, and to Vicka when she is well enough to come, three times a week. Now they meet her only on Monday and Friday nights. Mary tells them the place and time during the regular evening apparition at about 5.45. Monday nights, people can come. Friday nights are for only the group of about 15 young people; outsiders do not go to the Friday night meeting.

The prayer group of about 60 persons, with Tomislav Vlasic as chaplain, meets three evenings a week now, from 7.30 to about 9.30. Our Lady guides this group through Jelena and Marijana.

And Mary guides a smaller group, called the 'little group' *(mala grupa)* — about 13 young people going in age from Jelena as the youngest up to 23 years old that meets at Jelena's house every day at four in the afternoon for an hour. Mary guides this group with a quite firm hand, inviting people, through Jelena, to belong to it.

Both groups remain closed to outsiders; they are not at all 'open' prayer groups. What is their future? Where are they going? What will they turn into?

• *The church at Medjugorje.*

4. Jelena and the 'little group'
(January 1-2, 1986)

by Robert Faricy

January 1, Wednesday. We've had rain for several days now. Puddles in the road make the walking harder. The Lukoc river runs high and fast with muddy brown rapids.

This afternoon Sister Lucy and I will go with Father Pero to the daily prayer meeting of the 'little group' (it has no other name) at Jelena's. This is a very great privilege, as absolutely no outsider is ever permitted to go to that meeting. Father Pero acts as chaplain to the group.

Later: Pero and Lucy and I met in Marijana's bedroom with Jelena, Marijana, and nine other young women, most of them about 14 to 17 years old. They all seemed like ordinary girls, dressed in jeans or skirts, sweaters, and the other things girls their age all over the world wear. Jelena and Marijana both wear small gold crosses around their necks. The prayer meeting lasted from about 4.05 until about 5.10.

Jelena began it by reading a message about love that she had received from the Lord the night before. She had it written in a note book. Then they shared how they felt about the message, sharing one at a time with no comments or discussion. Next they sang a hymn. Immediately after the hymn Jelena gave what sounded like a prophecy, even though in the car afterward Pero called them 'interior locutions'. Lucy thinks maybe she's really hearing interior locutions and then speaking them. I would call that a form of prophecy.

Jelena began the prophecy with the words 'Jesus says' *(Isus kaze),* and the content, brief, followed. Another sharing, on the prophetic message, took place. No comments on what each said, no discussion.

Then another hymn. Another prophecy by Jelena, starting with 'Jesus says'. Another sharing in the same way.

Another hymn. A prophecy by Marijana — beginning again with 'Jesus says'. Another sharing. Then we all stood and sang the *Our Father* while holding hands in a circle. At the end of the prayer we fell to our knees and said a *Hail Mary* and a *Glory be*. The meeting was over. Pero spoke for a minute to Jelena and made an appointment for me at 10 tomorrow morning with Jelena and Marijana.

Then Lucy and I went on ahead of Pero to the car, got lost, ended up in Jelena's house where we met her father — graciously offering us wine and coffee — her little brother, and her wonderful grandmother. Jelena began to open up some Italian cake-bread *(panetone)*, but we saw Pero through the window waiting for us, and we left.

Pero and I talked in the car about the meeting. In these days, Pero said, all the messages are from Jesus. But often, in other times, it is Our Lady who gives messages through Jelena and Marijana.

Some things I wonder about: they did not use the Bible; no one read a Scripture text. They did not seem to keep a record of the prophecies; no one wrote them down. And, in my opinion, they spent much too little time praying.

The leader is clearly Jelena, even though she's the youngest. Pero comes sometimes, not always. His role seems to be that of chaplain.

January 2, Thursday. Jelena and Marijana are coming to the parish house this morning at 10 for an 'interview'. I know they hate interviews, and I do not plan on one. Instead we'll pray; then I'll give them my views on the prayer meeting and ask a couple of questions.

They are both 14 years old, a year younger than Jakov Colo, and close friends. Jelena is the leader; she has a strong character, and she tends to be withdrawn and aloof — but unafraid and never intimidated. Marijana is the quieter. She has what we used to call 'cool'. She chews gum often, and looks like she's on her way to a rock concert.

Those are my surface impressions. I'll have more, I hope, after the meeting with them. Sister Lucy will be there. Sister Janja will act as interpreter.

10.20 am. Jelena and Marijana came to the rectory. We met in the kitchen, where Lucy, Janja and I had just been talking with Mirjana. We went into the refectory and, after Jelena and Marijana put their gum in the wastebasket, sat at the dining-table to pray and to talk.

First, at Jelena's suggestion, we prayed seven *Our Fathers, Hail Marys, Glory be's*. Then I had a message, a prophecy really, about loving and reverencing the Lord, and loving and respecting other people. Lucy had a confirming text from the Letter to the Colossians. We prayed a little in silence.

Then I told them what Sister Lucy and I thought about the prayer meeting we attended yesterday. What we thought was good about it: clearly the Lord's work, well conducted, full of prayerfulness and love. And some suggestions: that they pray more and talk less; that not everyone has to share after every message from Jesus or Mary; and that other gifts will surely be given to the group, and some are already present but inactive — like the gift of finding the right text in Scripture.

Jelena explained that they talk a lot in the group because Jesus told them that the group is a school. They are there to learn. He teaches them through the messages and through their sharing. For example, yesterday evening the Lord taught them through four messages (prophecies, really) about love. And he taught them about love also through their own sharing. He taught them that he offers his love faithfully; but we have free will, and we can accept his love or not. Jelena said that yesterday in the meeting she was all overcome with Jesus' love.

After that I asked some questions: (1) Do the group members make a commitment? Answer: not a great commitment. It is to pray every morning, at noon, and to go to Mass daily or frequently during the week. And to love others.

(2) Do they know where the group is going? What is its future? Answer: to be a great sign of love in the world.

I told Jelena and Marijana that they could expect the group to suffer in the future. Jelena, who did almost all the talking during our meeting, said that the devil is always active, that Jesus told her the devil asked him for Medjugorje, the prayer group, the priests, and all who pray — to have those people in Medjugorje who pray — and Jesus could keep the rest of the world. Jelena feels that the future of the world depends somehow on what happens at Medjugorje. And that the eyes of the world are on Medjugorje.

The devil attacks, Jelena said, especially after times spent in prayer. She has to fight temptations, and she has to struggle to regain the love that the devil wants to take away from her.

When asked how they received the messages in and for the prayer group, whether a voice from outside, or a voice in their hearts, or words in their mind, they were at a loss to answer. Finally Marijana said she thought the Lord spoke to her in her heart. Jelena said she knows what happens but she can't explain it.

They agree that when they give messages in the prayer meetings it is Jesus or Mary who speaks to them. They have, then, a classic prophetic function in the prayer group. They are prophetesses in line with the New Testament prophets and prophetesses. Do they ever have visions during the prayer meeting? Sometimes. Even often. They see Jesus or Mary. They used to see them in visions 'in the heart', in an interior way. Now they both see Jesus and Mary 'outside' as it were.

Outside prayer meetings, at other times, they also have visions of Jesus or Mary, who speak to them. The message phenomenon, which seems to me to be a strong gift of prophecy, occurs only during the prayer meetings. But both of them see Jesus and Mary frequently, especially outside the prayer meeting, during the week. Sometimes they see Jesus or Mary at Mass after receiving Communion.

Sister Janja asked Jelena what Jesus looks like when she sees him in vision. Jelena replied that, especially when Jesus tells her that the world will not listen to his words, and when he says similar things, she feels so small and even tiny before him that she does not notice even the colour of his hair.

Jelena told Sister Lucy and me that we should be grateful to the Lord for the graces the Lord has given to us.

After a little over an hour we finished, and the two girls left the rectory. They are remarkable, and quite different. Jelena is very shy. She looked at Janja, not at me, when she spoke; and even when I spoke to her, she did not look at me. Jelena has an even stronger character than I thought, determined, decisive, with no hint of anxiety or desire to please. A straight manner, no falseness or pretence. And yet quite charming, gracious, and above all transparently humble. She has high intelligence and seems articulate.

Jelena has a pretty face, her hair pulled back with bangs (I think they're called) in front.

Jelena seems to me to have considerable spiritual maturity. Not just a maturity beyond her years, but beyond what the majority of Christians, including priests and religious ever attain. Slavko has told me that at the end of November she went through an intense spiritual desert, led by the Lord but unable to pray at all in any situation. During this desert time she had no visions at all. The fruit of this difficult experience: a strong desire for prayer. 'Now,' she says, 'I know what prayer is.'

I find it hard to described Marijana because she speaks so little. A good-looking girl, slender, shy but not as shy as Jelena. Marijana looked at me frequently when I spoke. She moves more slowly than the heavier Jelena, and has a matter-of-fact, down-to-earth air.

Jelena. Jelena Vasilj was born May 14, 1972, in Medjugorje.[1] She lives with her parents, her grandparents, and her five brothers and sisters. Jelena is the second oldest. The family have always prayed together and individually, but since Jelena began having visions and locutions, they pray more.

Jelena's father, Grgo, and her mother, Stefica, are simple people, hard-working, with a deep faith. They ordinarily attend Mass every evening. They stay after Mass for the prayer of the sick, because they understand it as a prayer for all the gifts, and especially for the healing of faith, hope, and love. They take part in parish activities. The family pray together every morning and every evening.

Both her parents take Jelena's spiritual gifts quite seriously. They say Jelena has always been a quite normal child, without being extreme in any way. She is a good student; she likes school work, but she can be a little negligent about it. She likes to play. She has never had any special treatment or privileges from her parents.

They both say that, except for her spiritual gifts, Jelena does not stand out from her brothers and sisters.

Jelena's paternal grandparents, who live in the same house with her, agree that except for her gifts she is like all their grandchildren.

---

1. This section is based mainly on an unpublished paper by Father Slavko Barbaric, 'Phenomenological Comparative Account of the "Inner Locutions" of Jelena Vasilj and Marijana Vasilj.' The study has 86 pages and is dated October 1985.

Both grandparents go to church nearly every evening. And they both, like the parents, take Jelena's gifts seriously.

What is the relationship between Jelena and the six young people who saw or who still see Our Lady every day? Jelena is much younger than Marijana, Ivanka, Ivan, Vicka, and Marija, and has little contact with them, although both Jelena and Marija belong to the 'big prayer group' that has Tomislav Vlasic as chaplain. Jakov is a year older than Jelena, and they went to the same school until a year ago when Jakov transferred to the secondary school at Citluk; but they live in different parts of the parish and have different friends. The most important connection between Jelena and the six from Bijakovici is Our Lady.

Jelena's locutions began on December 15, 1982, in school, during biology class. In an interview with Father Tomislav Vlasic, she describes what happened. Here are excerpts from the interview.

Jelena: I was bored. I said to myself, 'I wonder what time it is.' Something said to me, 'Twenty minutes past ten.' I said to myself, 'What's going on?' I asked the girl next to me, 'Tanya, what time is it?' She said, 'Ten twenty.' I felt uncomfortable. I began to raise my hand to answer a question and the same voice said to me, 'Do not raise your hand, you will not be called on.' I laughed. I asked myself, 'What is going on?'

I told my friends what I had experienced, and that I was afraid. They said, 'Don't lie; God will punish you; you should go to confession for lying.' When I got home I told my Dad. He said that there are people like that; God gives them a gift to hear voices. I got scared and I was nervous. I felt like crying.

Later we were working with tobacco leaves, and suddenly a feeling of joy seized me; I felt like jumping ten feet in the air. I was so happy. I was so joyful. Then suddenly something, the same voice, asked me, 'Are you joyful?' I said, 'I am.' I was really happy. I couldn't stop it. I sang a lot. And I prayed to God, 'Thank you, God!'

I don't remember everything. I think now that I wasn't aware of how happy I was. Dad told me that you said that my happiness was a positive sign and that you would come to speak with me. I told Dad how happy I was, and he told me not to go around telling everyone what had happened, because who knows what it might be? But I didn't listen to Dad at all. I talked about it a lot. Someone comes and asks you what did you hear? What kind of voices do you hear? I talked about everything to anyone who asked me. For days I listened to the voice. I prayed within myself; there was always something drawing me to prayer, telling me to pray.

Before, I was afraid to go to confession. I was always afraid: the priest will punish me for my sins. From then on I was not afraid. We all went, me and my friends, to confession. We became different. Many were saying to me: 'Lucky you, dear, now you know that you will go to heaven.' It went on like that for a week. After a week, that was on December 23, my mother and I were praying and suddenly I saw an angel. I looked: What is this? He was asking us to pray, to fast, and saying that that was from God and that I shouldn't be afraid. So I wasn't afraid.

T: You were peaceful?

J: I was so peaceful and happy that what some said didn't bother me. I mean, before when someone would not answer my question I would always be hurt and I would run away, hide somewhere and cry. This time I was so happy. I was happy that they said it wasn't true. It was like that. Nothing could have stopped me. I was filled, as they say, I was full of the Spirit.

T: What did the angel look like?

J: The angel had a rosy robe. He was barefooted. He was about five or six or seven years old, something like that — small. The wings were upright and his hands were joined in prayer. He had short curly hair, and his face — I can never remember his face. Later he came in a blue robe. I could see that he was an angel, thinking that is the same angel, but in a different robe. He was happier. I asked the angel: 'Can I ever see Our Lady?' And I hadn't finished saying that when suddenly she appeared in front of me; she was all in white. She looked first toward heaven, then turned toward me and smiled. I was so happy. I was completely happy. This is the way the angel and Our Lady appeared: on the right hand side there was the angel standing, on the other, the left, Our Lady. That was December 29, 1982.

T: Now describe to me what Our Lady looks like when she appears to you.

J: She's all in white. The edges and bottom of her gown — I don't know how to explain it — are lined with golden colours. Her gown and the veil are in a glowing white. She has brown eyes and brown hair. Her face is rosy and she always smiles. Her hands are joined in prayer. Around her left hand she holds a brown rosary. She doesn't have a crown, only stars around her head.

T: What do you mean, doesn't have a crown? What does that mean?

J: It's not a crown, it doesn't have those — how should I put it? — wires.

In a later interview dated March 19, 1984, Jelena told Father Tomislav what Our Lady is like when she appears to her. Here is part of that interview.

T: Tell me what you notice about Our Lady.

J: I notice that sometimes she is happy, she is also sometimes sad, and that she cries often and that she wishes more people would pray.

T: When is she sad?

J: She is sad the most when people sin. She's sad on some feast-days, she is sad even on her greatest feast-days.

T: Does she look like any particular picture or a statue that you have seen before?

J: No. It is difficult to describe. She is much more beautiful than all the pictures or the statues, and her grace which she extends when she looks at you — she gives you some grace when she looks at you. I never noticed that when I looked at any statue. I could draw her, but her face I would never be able to draw.

T: Tell me, what do you feel when you see Our Lady? What do you feel inside?

J: When she is with me I am more glad; when she is sad, I am sad; when she is happy, normally I am glad.

From the beginning, the voice Jelena heard was Our Lady's voice, although she did not know that at first. Later on, one of Jelena's friends, Marijana Vasilj, received the same gift. Here is part of an interview Father Slavko Barbaric had with Jelena and Marijana.

Slavko: Jelena, after the beginning of the 'locutions' you began to pray more and to fast, but not alone. You prayed more with your family and also with your friends. How did it happen that Marijana came to be offered the same gift?

Jelena: We usually prayed together ever since I heard the voice. We prayed at least one hour every day. Before the apparitions we always used to have arguments. Later we somehow became united and we argued less. Precisely on the day on which we were supposed to pray, I called Marijana to come. She said to me that she was not going to come that day, that she was going to go home. Suddenly Our Lady asked me to call her. I had something in me against her; I was not able to love her. But Our Lady said to me again, 'Go and call her, I will give her a great gift.' I went. She was playing outside. She ran in front of me and asked: 'What is it? What do you want?' I said 'Our Lady asked you to come, she will give you a great gift.' She immediately came running. We reconciled and we prayed together. Our Lady gave her a little crucifix and she said that she will see her. She said to me: 'I see her.' It was like that.

S: What kind of crucifix was that?

Marijana: I see that crucifix with my eyes closed like I see Our Lady. She gave it to me in my hands. It is a simple crucifix. Only when I pray concentratedly do I see the crucifix. It helps me to concentrate.

J: She gave me a rosary once, when we were praying. That rosary is not seen by anyone but me. It is at home.It is something like, brown. She gave me the rosary off her hand. But immediately there was a rosary on her hand again.

Still later, in 1985, Slavko Barbaric interviewed Jelena and asked her quite precise questions in order better to determine the nature of her experience. The interview runs seven typed pages. Here are some excerpts from it.

S: Where do you hear the voice?

J: Somehow in the heart and in the head. I feel it like a fire in my heart.

S: How do the words come: one by one or as a stream?

J: When I am well concentrated, then they come one after the other fluently; and when I am poorly concentrated, then the words somehow struggle out.

S: Do you draw out the words or do they come by themselves or from someone, but only slowly?

J: They come by themselves. But they come from some obscure, unknown side. Some voices collide and with difficulty I hear that voice. But when I concentrate, then I hear.

S: Can anyone disturb you? Would you stop if I said to you during this time, 'Jelena, listen to me'?

J: I hear what others say, I would hear you too, but I wouldn't stop. I would soon forget what others have said.

S: You hear the voice. Do you see the pictures?

J: What do you mean pictures? It is not a picture that I see. I see Our Lady, but that is not of human form; that is something supernatural. I don't see her as I see other people. I can't see her at all if I am not at least fifteen minutes in prayer.

● *Fr Slavko Barbaric — questions.*   ● *Jelena — answers.*

S: Well, when you have prayed for fifteen minutes, how do you see her?

J: When I pray that little, I see her with more difficulty. But when, for instance, I pray for half an hour, then I see her easily; but at times, when I don't pray, even if she is coming to me, other things come to me and I do not see her clearly: this is Our Lady, this is not Our Lady. I have to concentrate. Without that it is like without Our Lady.

S: Does that depend only on your concentration or on a certain time? If you concentrate now, would you see her?

J: I see her at a certain time. Now I wouldn't see her. Our Lady says to me at what time she will come, and then after some prayer I see her.

S: Have you seen anyone else besides Our Lady?

J: I have seen the angels, Our Lady, Little Jesus, St Joseph, the Holy Family.

S: Do you see anyone you wish or does it somehow come by itself? For example, you wish and you say: 'Today I would like to see this'?

J: No. For example, I saw the Holy Family because Our Lady showed it to me. Our Lady, Joseph and Jesus came together. Once I wished to see the little angels and I saw them.

S: Do you wish that before the vision or during the vision?

J: Once I said to Our Lady during the vision that I would like to see something, and she showed me. Before the vision I didn't speak anything or wish anything. I saw Jesus on the cross, I saw Our Lady in tears with a blue veil, I saw the manger.

S: Tell me, what else did you see?

J: I saw the manger twice. This year for ten minutes, and the last year for a little more, almost half an hour.

S: When you see, do you pray and do you see with these natural eyes?

J: I don't pray then. I don't see with these natural eyes.

S: What does Our Lady look like?

J: She has a joyful, simple face; it is difficult to describe.

S: Is there anything else that you see?

J: I saw Jesus on the cross, Our Lady as she was crying...

S: Once you heard some terrible voice that scared you?

J: I heard that voice during the *Our Father* and I forgot the *Our Father*. The voice was saying to me: 'Don't; what do you need all that for, it is better for you not to listen to Our Lady!' All kinds of words were coming out. And I was praying and praying. And then I received the strength to continue the *Our Father*.

S: How do you explain that?

J: I think that that was a small temptation. Satan wanted to see if there was any hope left for him to take me away from God.

S: Satan?

J: Yes, that was him.

S: How do you know? Did Our Lady tell you anything about it?

J: No, I saw it myself from his conduct.

S: What is the difference when you listen to Our Lady and to that other voice?

J: When I hear Our Lady she speaks so peacefully; and that other voice is, like, ordering, like demanding. Our Lady said 'Pray', and then we pray. But he doesn't want to. He is like, speaking the words into emptiness; he demands, insists; all like he is quivering, waiting for an answer. Our Lady has never asked me whether I will pray or not. And he is like, as if he is waiting.

S: Where do those themes which you brought to me before Christmas come from?

J: Us. The small group was praying here. And I heard from the little Jesus those messages.

S: What does that voice sound like?

J: Like a little baby's. God adapts himself to us, to the way we are.

S: You receive messages, for whom?

J: For the big and little groups, for the parish, and for the whole world.

S: What does Our Lady ask from one and what from the other?

J: She asks the same; but from the little group in a more open manner because we have opened, and the large group is still closed. We in the little group are like sisters. In the big group no one ever wants to say anything, even when it is boring. Everyone becomes closed in himself. The difference is in the openness, but the goal is the same.

S: What is the goal?

J: The goal is to be closer to God, to serve him better.

S: What do you read?

J: Bible, school books...

S: Did you read *The Living Flame of Love*?

J: I have skimmed it, and I pick it up sometimes.

S: Do you receive messages more easily when you read the books?

J: No, I don't. I read that once a little bit (pointing to a book on Slavko's desk), and I forgot everything. I took that from the parish office, read it and brought it back. I do not know anything about those books, and I do not learn anything from them.

S: What is said to you in your religion classes?

J: Mainly like this, about culture, about the Church.

S: Do the homilies help you to hear the voice and the message?

J: I think it is my own fault that I do not fully concentrate at the Mass. I follow it and it is good then, but I forget and do not remember it during the day. But it has never happened that during the Mass there was a message from the voice. But there were times when the same thing was said in the homily as in a previous message that I had received before that homily. So Our Lady says something, and later someone talks precisely about that.

S: So, today you have a message and tomorrow the homily is on that theme?

J: Yes, that happens.

S: Did it ever happen that a priest says something, and then later the same thing is in the message?

J: As I remember now that hasn't happened.

S: When you remember your life before the visions and now, is there any difference?

J: There is. It was easier for me to accept humiliation before and now it's more difficult.

S: How is that? If it's more difficult for you to accept humiliation, does that mean that it is not a good voice; it doesn't build you up?

J: It does build me up! I have experienced that. That which used to accumulate in my heart now comes out. I used to think and wish different things about people. I would permit myself to be humiliated, but in my heart I thought all kinds of things. Now it is the other way around. Physically I react but in my soul it is easier for me to accept humiliation, easier for me to accept others. It is easier for me to accept others when I immediately react straightforwardly. When I say something nice, and later begrudge...I have said to myself: I do not want to accumulate anything in my heart. I will never do that. I used to accumulate: he is this, he is that way; but I will not do that. I say it immediately to your face, you are that way; and I will not think about it and I will not accumulate it.

S: Prayer now and before?

J: The experience of prayer has grown, but before I enjoyed prayer more than now.

S: Before it began?

J: No. I used to enjoy prayer more when I had just started.

S: And what about before?

J: Before, I also liked praying. But now I like praying when it's shorter and nice, more than when it's long and dragging.

S: What do you mean by shorter?

J: I mean around one hour...

S: Was that voice which was hollering similar to your Dad's voice or to someone's from the house?

J: Ah, come on, no! From my experience I became convinced that that was the voice of Satan and the other one is the voice of Our Lady. Let me say why: when she speaks then every word is in its proper place and she doesn't speak in vain like we ordinary people so often speak empty words and in vain. Every voice for example from God always speaks with some meaning. Speaks consciously. And we ordinary people speak empty words, words which are sometimes unnecessary to speak. That is happening all over. I myself still speak things sometimes with no meaning. But that voice is different. And something else: Our Lady would never say for sure 'Go and sin'. She hasn't experienced sin.

S: What does Our Lady wish from us?

J: Often people say that they wish to see Our Lady. Then I begin to think: if you really want to see Our Lady so that she helps you in life, that is good. But if you want to see her only for the sake of seeing her, then nothing will help you. When you see Our Lady, everything becomes clear to you. Often I wished that, and now I received that gift. But now I see that I was at great fault because I wanted to see her. That is how I feel on one hand because the one who sees Our Lady has many obligations. I must surrender to God's will; now I see that I am never supposed to ask for anything. Now I know that God ought to be the first and the most important.

The 'big group' began through Jelena and has been guided from the beginning by Our Lady speaking through Jelena and, later, also through Marijana. This guidance takes the form of messages before and after meetings and, especially, prophecies during the meeting. Our Lady encourages, reprimands, and leads the group. She gives specific practical instructions on prayer, reading scripture, reconciliation, community, and other topics relevant to the lives of the big group members.

Our Lady also leads the 'little group', through Jelena and Marijana. The little group began on August 27, 1984. Jelena, together with Marijana, Slavica, Stanka, Andrijana, and another Jelena, were praying in Stanka's bedroom; it was the only place they could find to pray together. The last name of all the girls is Vasilj, and they all live in the same part of the village of Medjugorje. They had prayed together often before.

This time, during their prayer, Jelena suddenly saw Jesus, Our Lady, and an angel. Our Lady began to lead them in praying the rosary. All present said they had never experienced such strong prayer. At the end Our Lady asked them to come again the next day for prayer. The next day Jelena was sick, so the others went to Krizevac with Marijana. Without expecting anything special they prayed. Suddenly, completely surprised, Marijana heard the voice of Our Lady speaking about a sinful world, about Satan who seduces, and about the need to pray much.

Slavica Vasilj keeps the records of the group. These are private, since they regard only the life of the group, and — as far as I can determine — consist mainly of messages and prophecies from Our Lady and from Jesus.

Each member of the group rises to pray at 5.30 am, then wakes the rest of her family later for morning prayer. They also pray during the day. And they meet from 4 to 5 every afternoon except towards the end of the school term when there are examinations, or when the work in the fields is particularly demanding and the girls need to work with their families for the grape or tobacco crops.

The group frequently visits the cross on Mount Krizevac. And the girls go to the evening Mass in the church. They all fast regularly, at least every Wednesday and Friday, on bread and water.

In October 1985, eight girls made up the group: the original six and two sisters, Ivanka and Ilijana Vasilj. When Sister Lucy and I prayed with the little group in January 1986, there were 13 girls in the group. So the group seems to be growing.

Here is a sampling of the messages that Jelena has received.

October 24, 1983. Our Lady said: 'Pray!' For the group she said: 'If you pray, a spring will rise in your hearts, a spring of life. If you pray vigorously, if you pray with faith, from that spring of life you will receive graces and your group will be stronger.'

October 26, 1983. Our Lady said: 'I pour out a special blessing upon you and my heart wishes to be with you.'

October 29, 1983. Our Lady said: 'I give you my heart. Receive it! I do not wish to be someone whom you continually reject and ignore. I want it to matter to you whether or not I am here. My heart wants to be with you. You must pray, and do not ever say: "It doesn't matter that we didn't pray today!" But you must embrace prayer. Prayer is the only way to peace. If you pray and fast, whatever you ask you will receive.'

October 30, 1983. Our Lady said this: 'Why don't you surrender to me? I know that you pray much; but truly surrender to me. Pray again this evening when you finish all your work. Sit in your room and say to Jesus: "Thank you!" There are so many people today who have departed from him. Pray to him that he give them the grace to return. Offer thanks to Jesus. Pray to him that he see you safe into the next day. Without prayer you will not get through.'

November 18, 1983. Our Lady said: 'There are many people in Medjugorje who have begun turning towards material goods, and they forget the only good. There is no prayer any more.' She said that she doesn't have anything against their having material goods but she is very sad in her heart because they go to ruin because of that. Some people are envious of those who have more. Therefore it is necessary to become free as much as is possible. She said 'Therefore pray. This is not to scold you. This is just a warning, an incentive for you to make one more step in your faith. Therefore pray.'

November 14, 1983. Our Lady said this: 'Pray, because prayer is life. Through it and in it you live.'

December 1, 1983. Our Lady said: 'Thank you for your gathering here to pray to Jesus in this cold and icy-bad weather. Persevere in endurance and patience. You know when a friend of yours asks you for something perseveringly, you grant it to him. Jesus does the same. When you pray unceasingly, coming persistently, he will grant you everything that you need. There-fore pray.'

December 2, 1983. Our Lady said: 'Thank you and thank you!' (This evening again was also unusually cold.) 'Be so good and come to Mass with no fear or reproach. Offer your hearts to me ceaselessly.' I recommended one sick person. Our Lady only answered: 'Just pray.'

February 1, 1984. Our Lady said: 'Now is the rainy season, and you say: "It is difficult to go to church because of the mud. Why does this rain continue? Why doesn't it stop?" Do not speak like that. You prayed that God give you rain so that your fields would be fruitful. So do not reject this blessing of God, but rather thank him with prayer and fasting.'

February 15, 1984. Our Lady said: 'The wind is my symbol. I come in the wind; when there is wind, know that I am with you. No, not in the same way as the cross is a symbol of Christ to put in your house. It means this: you come to church even when it is cold. You are willing to offer everything for God. Then I am with you. That is why I am with you in the wind. Do not be afraid.' (Today was exceptionally cold and windy. There were only about 250 people in the church.)

February 25, 1984. Our Lady said: 'Know that I love you. Know that you are mine. I do not wish to do for anyone more than I wish to do for you. Come to me. Be with me and I will be your mother forever. Come because I want to have each one of you.'

May 19, 1985. Our Lady said: 'Dear children, at this time it is especially necessary that you consecrate yourselves to me and to my heart.' Our Lady said: 'Love, pray and fast.'

May 21, 1985. Our Lady said: 'Oh, dear children, how much do I wish to convert you to myself. Imagine, my little children, it is the end of the school year and you haven't even come half-way. Therefore now you must become a little more serious.'

May 28, 1985. Our Lady said: 'Love is a gift of God. Pray therefore that God give you that gift so that you can love.'

June 1, 1985. Our Lady said: 'Let the love of God be always in you, because without it you cannot fully be converted. Let the rosary be in your hands as a remembrance of Jesus.' Our Lady said: 'Dear children, make an effort to understand the Mass the way you ought to.'

Two interesting and important communications came from Our Lady to Jelena during the 1984 Christmas season. The first occurred on the occasion of a visit to Jelena on the part of Archbishop Frane Franic of Split and Father Slavko. At one point in the conversation, Jelena said she had something to give them. She stood, left the room, and returned with a sheet of paper on which she had written nine themes for preaching for a Christmas novena. Our Lady had given them to her during the hour of prayer just before the visit. Here is the message from Our Lady and the nine sermon themes that were all on the sheet of paper.

Let the church be fragrant with Christmas. Let Christmas be already on your doorstep. Purify your hearts and be pure receiving Christmas. Do not let luxury be more important at Christmas than Jesus who is being born. Receive him with joyful hearts. Let everyone receive Christmas this way.

1. Open your hearts because Jesus wants to dwell in them after Christmas.

2. To accept Christmas with love.

3. To purify yourself for Christmas.

4. From now on let Jesus be first in your hearts.

5. Let only Jesus give you joy.

6. Let love be in your words.

7. The God-man who wants the whole world to be one has been born.

8. To live in Jesus.

9. Do not separate yourselves from Christmas.

The second communication of Christmas 1984 was a long vision. Jelena told Tomislav Vlasic the story, and Tomislav recorded it.

Here is a translation from the Croatian of part of the recording.

Jelena: A few days before Christmas a movie, *Ben Hur*, was playing in Citluk. They said that Jesus was mentioned in it, how he was born and how he suffered. The movie was starting at 7 pm. Marijana and myself were going to church every evening because Our Lady has asked this of us, and the rosary and prayers were after Mass. Because of that my Dad said to me that I couldn't see the movie. I was sad for that reason.

Then Our Lady said to me: 'Do not be sad. On Christmas I'll show you how Jesus was born.' (Those Christmas days an angel was appearing to me as in the previous year.) This was how the vision went: I see an angel. Then he disappears and I see darkness. In that darkness I see St Joseph. He holds a staff in his hands. In that place there is some grass, and stones on the road, and a few houses around. Mary is on a mule. It looks like she is crying but she is not crying. She is sad. She says, 'I would be glad if someone would take us in for tonight, because I am tired.' Joseph says, 'Here are the houses; we will ask.' And they knock at doors. Mary stands in front of the house. Joseph knocks on the door. People open the door, and when they see Joseph and Mary they close it. That is repeated two or three times. When they start towards the other houses the lights begin disappearing in them. They are sad. Joseph says, 'There, there is an old house; surely no one sleeps in it. Surely it's abandoned.' And they go there. Inside there is one mule. They put their own mule alongside the manger. Joseph gathers some pieces of wood and they make a fire. He also puts some hay in it but the fire consumes it immediately. So Mary is warmed more by the mule. Mary cries and is very sad. Joseph feeds the fire. Suddenly I see Jesus in front of Mary. He smiles as if he were one year old. He is joyful, and it seems as if he is speaking. He waves his hands. Joseph comes to Mary and Mary says, 'Joseph, this day of joy has come, but it would be better to pray, because there are people who do not allow Jesus to be born.' So they pray.

Suddenly I see a little house only. It is lighted up a little bit. And then suddenly it becomes completely lighted up as in daytime, and the stars are in the skies. I see two angels above the stall. They hold a big banner, and written on it is: 'We glorify you, Lord!' Above it there is like a big choir of angels. They sing and glorify God. Then I see the shepherds. They are weary, tired, and some are already sleeping. Some walk. The sheep and lambs are with them. One angel approaches them and says, 'Shepherds, hear the good news! God is born! You will find him sleeping in a manger in the stall. Know that

I am telling you the truth.' Suddenly a large choir of angels joins them singing.

Tomislav; Did you look at this as in a movie?

Jelena: It looked real. I looked at that as I look at Our Lady.

Here are accounts of two other visions that Jelena has had. Jelena is speaking, describing the visions.

I saw Satan as he was walking above a group, forging his plans. I heard him speaking: 'Some I will try to throw out of the group, some I will cool down. Those who are interested in movies and other things on television — I will satisfy them, and I will give money to those working at studios to show more on television. I will let them watch it and I will disturb prayer. I will put that on after Mass so that they run home and watch it. I will try to mellow them.' Our Lady said, 'He leaves many people in order to take over the group. These days he especially attacks the visionaries and the priests, and he has already made the bishop angry. He has left many, many people in order to take over our Medjugorje.'

Our Lady showed me a white road. There was a fork in the road. On one side there was written *life* and on the other *death*. Our Lady was standing next to the road of death, and she was stopping people so that they wouldn't go to their death. One man was walking toward death and he saw no one following him and he returned. Another man also walked toward death and many people after him. Our Lady couldn't make him return. And they went to death. Our Lady said, 'Always, when no one follows the person who sins, that sin will be uprooted. But if you follow that person, the sin will spread.'

Here are two prayers, both dictated to Jelena by Our Lady on June 22, 1985. Jelena explains the first prayer according to what Our Lady told her about it. The prayer asks for God's mercy, that it come upon us, that God be good to us. The last part of the prayer Jelena explains this way: it is as when a little child might tell his brother, 'Tell Dad to be good to me, and that I love him and I'll be good.'

A cry to God

O God,
My heart is in distant depths,

But still it is bound up with your Heart.
My heart can be torn between you and Satan.
Do not allow that!
And always, when it is divided
Between good and evil,
Let your light shine upon me,
So that my heart is whole.
Don't ever allow
Two loves to dwell in me,
Let there never be two faiths in me,
And never let come together in me lies and truthfulness,
Love and hate,
Honesty and dishonesty,
Humility and pride.
But let my heart
Be raised like a child before you,
So that it brings peace,
For which it should always yearn.
Let your holy will and your love
Find a dwelling in me,
Who at least sometimes wish to be your child.
And then, Lord,
When I do not wish to be that,
Remember my desires of old
So that I can accept you once again.
I open my heart to you;
Let your holy love stay in it.
I open my soul to you;
Let your holy mercy touch me —
So that I clearly realise my sins,
And that it is sin which blemishes me.
I wish to be your child, God,
Humble and true,
And through that sincere loving,
A child that a Father can cherish.
Help me, Jesus, my brother,
That your Father be good to me
And that I be good to him.
Help me, Jesus, to understand well
What the Father gives me,

Because sometimes I do not do good
Because I understand it as evil!

The second prayer, Jelena says, not only came to her from Our Lady but is recommended by Jesus himself. Jesus asks, says Jelena, that both the sick person and the one praying for the sick person should surrender to God through this prayer.

Prayer for a sick person

O, my God,
This sick person who is before you
came to ask you for that
which he sees as most important: that which he desires,
sees it as being most important to him.
But you, God,
bring into his heart these words:
'It is important to be healthy in soul!'
Lord,
Let your holy will be done
upon him in everything!
If you will it,
Let him receive the healing.
If it is your will
Let him continue bearing his cross.
I pray to you for us,
who are praying to you for him;
purify our hearts that we become worthy
that you give your holy graces through us.
Guard him and lighten his pains.
Let your holy will continue to be fulfilled upon him,
and grant that your holy love manifest itself in him.
Help him to carry his cross courageously.

(After this prayer, say the *Glory be* three times.)

Finally, here is how Our Lady taught Jelena, Marijana, Andrijana, and Slavica a way to pray the *Our Father*. The four girls were praying together, and Our Lady taught them through Jelena. The following then are the words of Our Lady speaking to Jelena.

Our! Our Father! He is our Father. Why are you afraid of him? Extend your hands to him. Our Father means: he gave himself to you as a father. He gave you everything. You know that your father would do everything for you, and how much more your heavenly Father?

Father! Whose Father is he? Where is that Father?

Who art in heaven! Father, who art in heaven. That means: your earthly father loves you but your heavenly Father loves you many times more than your father here. Your father becomes angry sometimes, but he doesn't. He only gives you love.

Hallowed be thy name! In return you must respect him, for he gives everything to you and is Father to you; you must love him. You must hallow and praise his name. Before sinners you must say: He is the Father and a real Father and I will serve him and praise only his name. That is the formula — hallowed be thy name.

Thy Kingdom come! That is the formula of our thanks to Jesus. Say to him: 'Jesus, we know nothing without your Kingdom; we are weak without you. Our kingdom is a disaster. It is perishable, but yours is not. Bring it to us.'

Thy will be done! O Lord, let our kingdom go to ruin so that yours becomes true. Let us realise now that our kingdom will be ruined so that we immediately at the beginning allow your will to be done.

On earth as it is in heaven! That shows, Lord, how the angels listen to you, how they respect you. Let us also be able to do that. Let our hearts be opened and enable our hearts to respect you as do the angels. Grant that everything on earth be done in as holy a way as it is in heaven.

Give us this day! Give us, Lord, bread and food for our soul. Give it to us now, give it to us today, give it to us always. Let that bread be food for our soul. Let that bread feed us. Let that bread hallow you, let that bread be eternal.

Our daily bread! Lord, we beg you for our bread. O Lord, let us be able to receive it. O Lord, what shall we do? Let us realise that we will not receive our daily bread without prayer.

And forgive us our trespasses! And forgive us our trespasses. Forgive us, Lord, our trespasses! O, forgive us because we are not good, because we are not faithful.

As we forgive those who trespass against us! Forgive us because we will forgive those whose sins we were not able to forgive before. O Jesus, forgive us we beg you!

And lead us not into temptation! Lord, free us from difficult temptations. Lord, we are weak. O Lord, do not let those temptations be a ruin for us.

But deliver us from evil! Lord, deliver us from evil. Let us feel only a grace in those temptations, one more step into life.

Amen! Let it be that way, Lord, and let your will be done.

5. Mirjana (January 2, 1986)

by Robert Faricy

Just before our meeting with Jelena and Marijana, at 9.55 am, Mirjana came into the kitchen. She had come from Sarajevo to the village of Bijakovici yesterday to see Father Pero. And she came to the parish house for an interview with Father René Laurentin. Since she had come early for the interview, Sister Lucy and I had a chance to meet her — for the first time for us both — and to talk with her through Sister Janja as interpreter. We talked until 10.20, when Mirjana had her interview with Father Laurentin in the apparitions room, the office-bedroom of Father Ivan and Slavko, and when Jelena and Marijana came into the kitchen for their meeting with us.

Mirjana will give a full written report of what has happened to her in the past few months to Father Pero tonight at Mass. For some time now she has been having locutions from Our Lady about once or twice a month. In these locutions Mirjana hears Our Lady's voice speaking to her. On November 30 and again on December 25 Our Lady appeared to her and spoke to her. Both apparitions were, so to speak, by appointment. Our Lady had told Mirjana ahead of time, by a locution lasting a few minutes, the date and time of the apparition. The content of the apparitions concerned the 10 secrets, the first secret in particular, and the secrecy of these secrets. On Christmas day, Mary told Mirjana not to be afraid; God is our Father and Mary is our Mother. Your parents will not hurt you.

Late in 1984, Our Lady gave to Mirjana a rolled-up kind of parchment, something between cloth and paper, unlike any material Mirjana has ever seen. On the parchment, as Mirjana received it, are written the 10 secrets in Croatian. No one, of course, has read them except Mirjana. Pero can read the first secret, only 10 days before the date that it will be fulfilled.

She says that if she did not have special help from Our Lady she would sometimes go mad. She lives in Sarajevo in the midst of an almost completely secular society, and she lives with fear. She has seen the devil. She knows all 10 secrets. I get the impression that her family gives her less than a strong support in her religious convictions and in carrying all the weight of having been chosen to be visited by Our Lady, to have seen the devil, and to know all 10 secrets.

Mirjana is an attractive young woman in her early twenties, well and smartly dressed, her blonde hair stylish. One would never guess that she speaks face to face with the Blessed Virgin Mary. Quite different from Vicka and Marija, who are simple country girls. Mirjana is a city girl, poised and confident. And yet, as Sister Lucy pointed out to me, she has the same kind of spiritual beauty in her face that Marija and Vicka have and that, in a less mature way, Jelena and Marijana show in their faces.

Late in the morning, just before lunch, I met with René Laurentin to compare and share notes. I told him in detail about our meeting with Jelena and Marijana. And he shared with me his notes from his interview with Mirjana.

Father Laurentin found Mirjana less tense than he has found her before, relaxed, assured, peaceful, smiling easily. She shows no fear, and says that we should not be afraid of the secrets. Most of them are bad news, true. But God is our Father, Jesus is our Brother, and Mary our Mother; we do not need to be afraid. We can be glad, not with the happiness the world gives but with the joy that comes from the Lord.

Father Laurentin asked Mirjana why the apparitions are going on such a long time. Because, she answered, God wants to allow more time for sinners to be converted. When René Laurentin suggested it was a delay due to the patience of God, Mirjana agreed.

I ate noon meal with the sisters. The priests are all out in the villages of the parish blessing homes at the beginning of the new year according to the custom in Hercegovina. Now, as I write this after lunch sitting at the desk in the religious goods store, a small room across the hall from the office-bedroom of Ivan and Slavko, they greet me as they come in one by one, late for lunch. They will eat, rest a short time, and go out again.

Here is tonight's message from Our Lady to the parish:

Dear children! I invite you to decide completely for God. I beg you, dear children, to surrender yourselves completely and you will be able to live everything I say to you. It will not be difficult for you to surrender yourselves completely to God. Thank you for responding to my call.

Since the message came during the apparition, by the time Marija had written it and Fathers Pero and Ivan had typed it in Croatian and translated it into German it was already 6.20. The Mass had begun at 6. I spent the rest of the Mass in the sacristy translating the message into English, French, and Italian. Working through the message in four languages is a good way to 'hear' it, to understand it, to let it sink in.

Tomislav Pervan told me in the sacristy, while I was translating, that the message lacks a certain logic; there is no reason or basis given for the second last sentence. *Why* will it not be difficult for us to surrender completely? It upset him a little. I like the lack of perfect logic. This message, like all of them, has a from-the-heart simplicity. Not literary, it uses only a few words, repeating key words. Not a 'message', it's more like someone talking to you. It *is* someone talking to you. Not to your head only or even mainly, but to your heart.

• *Fr Pero Ljubicic — chosen by Mirjana as the priest to whom she will tell Our Lady's 10 secrets.*

6. Father Tomislav Vlasic (January 3, 1986)

by Robert Faricy

This afternoon at two, Sister Lucy and I will go to Vitina, to the parish rectory where Father Tomislav Vlasic lives. He has not been well, and he has not come here to Medjugorje for several days now. So we'll go there. Sister Lucy will say hello to Tomislav and leave; I'll stay and we'll talk.

We will certainly talk about the relationship between the bishop and the Franciscans involved in Medjugorje. In particular, we'll talk about two meetings with the bishop, both called by him. The first took place on Thursday, November 28, when Bishop Zanic called to his episcopal offices in Mostar the pastor here, Father Tomislav Pervan; Fathers Ivan and Petar (Pero); Sister Janja; and Marija, Ivan, and Jakov. The bishop spoke to this group about Father Tomislav Vlasic, and made very strong charges against him. The accusations against Father Tomislav upset Jakov greatly; he cried profusely in the bishop's office, and remained visibly upset for several days. In fact, the accusations upset everyone, and they are still upset.

Some time before this meeting, Bishop Zanic, according to a high source in the Yugoslavian church, told all the Yugoslavian bishops the same accusations he repeated to the Medjugorje group on November 28. I do not know whether he spread these charges by letter or in person at some kind of bishops' meeting. Apparently Bishop Zanic has related the same accusation to other people who have visited him in Mostar.

Then, Sunday morning at a little after ten, I have an appointment with Bishop Zanic. I'm going to see the bishop especially because most of the people who talk to him about Medjugorje speak strongly against it. Some of them are mentally ill, disturbed persons who project their inner conflicts and hatreds onto the main people — the Franciscans and the young people who see Mary — here at Medjugorje. I want to see him because I think some sane people who know about Medjugorje should also talk to him.

In the past few days I have met here around the church, for example, a young Frenchman extremely disturbed with what I take as marked symptoms of paranoia. He accosted me near the church and shouted questions at me about why I tolerated the disobedience to Bishop Zanic on the part of the Franciscan priests here. When I refused to answer, he yelled that he would not waste his time with me, and he stalked away. I discovered later that he is Bishop Zanic's house-guest in Mostar.

Stephen L, of New York City, has informed me that, while he respects my own belief in the authenticity of Medjugorje, he knows with certainty that the apparitions here are a CIA plot: the CIA has planned the whole thing from the beginning and carried it out with typical cunning and expertise. Stephen will report what he knows to the bishop in Mostar.

These are the people that talk to Bishop Zanic about Medjugorje. They reinforce his suspicions.

Later: Sister Lucy and I are waiting in the dining/living room of the parish house in the village of Vitina, about 20 minutes by car from Medjugorje, the other side of Ljubuski, a town somewhat larger than Citluk. Tomislav Vlasic lives here with two other Franciscan priests — the pastor and another curate — three Franciscan sisters who cook and keep house, and a small black cat.

Telephone communication between the Vitina and Medjugorje parish houses has proved impossible for the past few years, since Tomislav was transferred here from the Medjugorje parish. It seems certain this is the work of the local authorities.

Tomislav is resting now. Pilgrims to Medjugorje frequently stop to see him and speak with him, especially Italian pilgrims, since he speaks fluent Italian. Just before Lucy and I came, several car-loads and a whole bus full of Italians came to see him; when they left he went to his room for a short nap. He'll be down in a minute.

Later: Father Tomislav and I talked upstairs in his room. We are old friends and priests, so we ministered to one another and talked in a personal way. We talked for a long time. At one point, when it was getting late, I said that I had come to see him personally as a friend, not really for an interview. He said: 'I'll give you one anyway.'

So I took Sister Lucy's tape-recorder out of my pocket and taped what Tomislav said. Here it is.

Our Lady has told us not so much to give testimony directly, saying 'Here are Our Lady's words, here are her messages', but to carry her words in us so that when others see our gifts they will want to be like us. She has said we should live the messages with humility; it's enough that the world see the light shining out of our lives.

She has told the priests in the parish at Medjugorje: 'Dedicate yourselves to the parishioners.' There is no need to explain so much to those from outside the parish; they need to receive living witness from the parishioners.

Not words, but to enter into the mystery and to let our light shine out. We have enough words in the Gospel, in the Bible, but those are dead words for me unless there is light in me, unless I live those words and let them shine out of me in my life.

Whoever tries to defend Medjugorje with human logic has already lost the battle. Medjugorje is a mystery! Look what happens: when we use human force, then we provoke human force against us. Arguments give rise to more arguments. Arguments do not convince others, they do not lead to peace because they do not change the heart.

I can say this: when I found myself in all these difficulties and I didn't know what to do, I protested to Our Lady. She told me through Jelena: 'You do not know the power of God! Do not lose time writing letters to yourself. *Pray and love!*'

Before that, when the bishop forbade me to preach during the Masses at Medjugorje, I asked Our Lady through Jelena: 'What can I do to serve you, in Medjugorje and in my parish?' She answered: '*Love; love is enough*. If you love through Jesus it will not be hard to move people.' Then I grew in awareness that through love I can move people. By arguments I only upset myself.

I try to enter as deeply as I can into this message to me from Our Lady. I try to go forward now in silence, in that silence of God that puts all things in order according to the light of the Gospel. I can't go forward without that silence.

Another message from Our Lady that has helped me much came to our prayer group: 'Close your ears to many words. Turn to my words and to the words of my Son.' I understood from this that a lot of merely human words can be, humanly speaking, good and right and logical. But for me they are useless, even dangerous, because they feed something merely human in me. And I need to be completely united with Jesus.

• *On the statue of Our Lady, 'mir' — the Croatian word for peace.*

7. Bishop Pavao Zanic
(January 4-5, 1986)

by Robert Faricy

January 4, Saturday. Sister Lucy left early today for Rome. Angela telephoned this morning from Parma to say that an international medical commission will arrive in Medjugorje today or tomorrow. Four or five doctors of various nationalities, accompanied by an Italian industrialist. They intend to do some kind of medical study of the four young people who see Our Lady.

At the point in the conversation where I asked Angela whether or not the Bishop of Mostar knows about the arrival of this commission, we were cut off. Angela was gone, off the line. And I could hear not the dial tone but breathing. The breathing of whoever had listened and then cut us off. Spooky. I told him in Croatian that he had bad manners, and I hung up.

As I was speaking to Marija in the kitchen of her home, the medical commission arrived. I asked Marija what they would do. She said: 'Psychiatric examinations.' And she added: 'Our Lady has told us that the medical and psychological examinations do not serve any useful purpose.' So I asked: 'Then why do you let them do it?' She just shrugged helplessly.

I caught a ride back to the parish house, where I informed Father Slavko of what had happened and what I think about it. Slavko had known the commission was coming. They will report their conclusions to Bishop Zanic.

As we were talking, Slavko's pastor came into the parish house dining room to announce that the Franciscan provincial in Mostar wants to see Slavko immediately. So the two left in the pastor's car for Mostar. Apparently the strange and disturbed Frenchman has already reported Slavko to the bishop, and the bishop has spoken to the provincial.

Later: Slavko has returned. The Franciscan provincial asked him not to spend so much time at Medjugorje, to spend more time in his own parish and giving retreats and talks outside his parish and outside Medjugorje.

After the apparition was over and the medical commission, plus the other observers, were leaving the apparitions room, I recognised Bishop Hnilica, SJ. He is a leader of the commission, and he explained to me its purpose. It makes sense. This is a distinguished and reputable international commission of psychiatrists. Their examination of the four young people who see Mary will preclude a psychiatric examination by less well qualified and perhaps even prejudiced psychiatrists. I see the point. But I do feel that all these examinations put an unnecessary burden on Marija, Jakov, Vicka, and Ivan.

January 5, Sunday. At 8.45 this morning Jozo Vasilj took me in his taxi from Medjugorje to the bishop's residence in Mostar. Cost: five dollars. Ushered immediately into the bishop's dining room, I found him waiting for me. We spoke for about an hour. As he always has with me, the bishop showed great hospitality and cordiality. And respect for my belief in Medjugorje.

But he finds it nearly unbelievable that a Roman professor of spirituality can believe as I do. He does not at all see how, in face of all the ambiguities, in face of the apparent human weaknesses of persons involved in the events, and in face of the fact that the bishop himself stands accused by some of the things the Blessed Virgin Mary is supposed to have said, I can continue to believe in the authenticity of the Medjugorje apparitions. He added that Archbishop Franic of Split, and many others, have calumniated him.

Bishop Zanic did, however, seem much calmer and more serene than I have seen him before. He has aged considerably in the past few years. He looks older than his age; he is 67. But he remains vigorous of mind and body.

He did not get excited even when we spoke about the notorious problem of the Franciscan parishes in his diocese. The Holy See has repeatedly asked the Franciscan province of Hercegovina to hand over some or all of the parishes that remain staffed by Franciscans, even though there are enough diocesan priests now to man them. The Franciscans refuse to cede even one parish.

I asked the bishop why he did not simply take over some parishes, in the light of the fact that he is authorised to do so by the Holy See. He then spoke to me about people ready to murder him if he did such a thing. There are, he said, persons prepared to kill him.

What about the official diocesan commission that Bishop Zanic has named to investigate the events at Medjugorje? The bishop assured me, speaking with great confidence, that very soon the commission will issue a negative evaluation, concluding that the apparitions are false.

However, the bishop had assured me of the same thing when I spoke to him about a year ago. A unanimous negative conclusion on the part of the commission seems extremely unlikely even in the remote future. And it seems an impossibility in the near future.

On May 2, 1986, Rome took the matter of Medjugorje out of the hands of Bishop Zanic and into its own hands. In the whole history of Marian apparitions, this action has no precedent. The diocesan commission has been dissolved without ever making a decision or a report. Instead, each member gave the bishop six or seven pages stating how he judged the matter of the Medjugorje apparitions. The bishop has sent this material to the Sacred Congregation for the Doctrine of the Faith.

What will Rome do? The Sacred Congregation for the Doctrine of the Faith, under Cardinal Josef Ratzinger, now has charge of Medjugorje as to the apparitions there. It seems to be quite unlikely that Cardinal Ratzinger will appoint a new commission before the apparitions have ceased to occur daily. Once Ivan, Vicka, Jakov and Marija no longer see Our Lady daily, the Congregation may well appoint an international commission to study the matter.

Why did Rome take the whole affair out of the jurisdiction of the local bishop? The Pope is known to want to keep Medjugorje open to pilgrims. Perhaps Rome was afraid Bishop Zanic would close it down as a place of pilgrimage. Perhaps it feared that the diocesan commission would issue a negative verdict as to the authenticity of the apparitions. And perhaps both.

8. Evaluating Medjugorje

by Robert Faricy

Bishop Zanic let me read a Latin document from the Holy See. More precisely, from the Sacred Congregation for the Doctrine of the Faith, now headed by Cardinal Ratzinger. The document is dated February 25, 1978, and is signed by the then head of the Congregation, Cardinal Seper. It gives the positive and negative criteria for evaluating religious apparitions, and the conditions for interventions on the part of the Holy See and on the part of the relevant national conference of bishops.

Since the document is *sub secreto,* it cannot be photocopied or published in a book or magazine or newspaper. So I could not make a copy, and I cannot reproduce the four-page document here. But I can describe what I read in the bishop's dining room.

The title: *Norms of the Sacred Congregation for the Doctrine of the Faith about How to Proceed in Judging Alleged Apparitions and Revelations.* I find the document well balanced, concise, and admirable in every way. It begins by describing the origin and character of the norms it proposes to state. Today, the mass media promulgate information about alleged apparitions rapidly. And the ease of travel today makes it easy for pilgrims to visit places where apparitions are said to take place. On the other hand, it is difficult if not impossible to arrive at a judgment with due speed, a judgment about the authenticity of the apparitions (*'constat de supernaturalitate, non constat de supernaturalitate'*) so as to give the local bishop the possibility of permitting or forbidding a public cult or other devotional practices at the place of the apparitions. For these reasons, and so that the devotion of the faithful can be in full communion with the Church regarding facts of this kind, and so that the

Church from the time of the document on can have an instrument to determine the nature of the facts, the document lays down some criteria for evaluating apparitions and some norms for action regarding them.

The basic plan of action stipulated by the Congregation for the local ecclesiastical authorities has three stages: (1) to judge the facts according to positive and negative criteria set down later in the document; (2) then, if this results in a favourable judgment, to permit some manifestations of public devotion and worship, and to do so prudently, letting it be understood that for the time being there is no obstacle to public devotions and worship regarding the alleged apparitions; (3) then, in the light of experience over a certain length of time, especially of experience of spiritual fruit and of new devotion, if the case so warrants, a judgment of truth and of heavenly origin can be made.

Here are the positive and negative criteria for judging at least the probability of the truth and divine origin of apparitions. The first positive criterion is a moral certitude or at least a high probability, after a serious investigation, that the facts are as claimed. Secondly, particular circumstances are important. The personal qualities of the person or persons having the apparitions must be assessed as to psychological balance, honesty and good morals, sincerity, a respectful attitude toward Church authority, and so on. The theological and spiritual doctrine involved must be true and free from error. Finally, healthy religious devotion and spiritual fruits are positive signs; for example a spirit of prayer, conversions, and so on.

The negative criteria for a preliminary judgment about the apparitions are these. There should be no obvious error about the facts. There should be no doctrinal errors attributed to God or to Our Lady or to a saint. The document refers to the *Spiritual Exercises* of Saint Ignatius Loyola, number 336, which points out that even when something has a truly supernatural origin, human error — sometimes unconsciously — can creep in.

A further negative criterion, which would cast doubt on the authenticity of the apparitions, would be if money-making (*lucro*) is somehow involved in the events. Also, gravely immoral acts on the part of persons involved in the apparitions, mental illness, psychopathic tendencies, or psychoses, would point to an unfavourable judgment. So would evidence of collective hysteria or things of that kind.

The document states that these criteria are indicative, not absolute. And that they are cumulative and their application can result in certain converging lines of evidence.

After listing the criteria for a first assessment of the nature of the facts, the document goes on to talk about responsibility and authority regarding the apparitions. In the first place, the competent ecclesiastical authorities have a grave obligation to keep themselves informed on the matter and to carefully watch over what goes on. Also, the competent authorities can give permission to the faithful to practise certain forms of worship and devotion that derive from the apparitions. And the authorities can promote these devotions and ways of worshipping. They should intervene to correct abuses in devotional practices, to condemn any errors in doctrine, to guard against any false mysticism, and so on.

In doubtful cases, the competent ecclesiastical authorities should abstain from every judgment and direct action. But they should nevertheless watch over what happens and, if necessary, they can intervene promptly and prudently.

Who are these 'competent authorities'? First of all, the local ordinary; that is, the bishop of the diocese. Regional and national bishops' conferences can intervene if the local ordinary refers the matter to them, or if the matter has a regional or national importance. The Holy See can intervene when asked to do so by the local bishop, or if a qualified group of the faithful ask it to, or simply on its own in virtue of the universal jurisdiction of the Pope. In fact, the Holy See did so intervene when it took the whole matter of Medjugorje into its own hands on May 2, 1986.

What about the Sacred Congregation for the Doctrine of the Faith? Where does it come in? In its last section, the document details the Congregation's role, which can be quite great. The Sacred Congregation can intervene when asked to do so by the local bishop, or by a qualified group of the faithful, or simply on its own if the matter affects a large segment of the Church (as it did on May 2, 1986). Furthermore, the Sacred Congregation for the Doctrine of the Faith can study the matter either by itself or by means of appointing a special commission. At present, the Congregation follows closely events at Medjugorje, and may later appoint an investigating commission.

How does Medjugorje look in the light of this 1978 document from the Vatican? It certainly manifests the changes in the world that make the document necessary. The mass media from the beginning, first in Italian, then in English, then in other languages, have made Medjugorje an international fact known to the entire Catholic Church and beyond the Church. And, in spite of the inaccessibility of Medjugorje, pilgrims, especially from Europe, find their way here in increasing numbers.

How have the local ecclesiastical authorities followed the general action plan set out by the document? Unfortunately the Bishop of Mostar has not followed the plan of the document. The basic plan of action stipulates a preliminary judgment according to the criteria set out in the document. This is an official although preliminary statement. If favourable, investigation continues toward a more definitive judgment. Bishop Zanic, however, has not made this preliminary judgment, even though the apparitions have taken place daily for about five years. The bishop has not made *any* official statement about the events at Medjugorje. He has made some unofficial public statements marked by intemperate language and a highly unofficial emotional style. But never an official statement, and not the first judgment called for by the Vatican document.[1]

Bishop Zanic's appointed commission, apparently, had this task. But their work was incredibly slow and the results both confused and confusing. So the first step of the plan of action was not taken by the local authorities.

How do the Medjugorje events look in the light of the criteria given by the Vatican for making a first judgment? The first positive criterion, that the facts are as claimed, is easily applied. Something certainly is going on. The basic facts, that a small group of young people claim to see and speak with Our Lady daily, and that they receive messages from her as well as personal guidance, are clearly substantiated.

---

1. See especially Bishop Zanic's document: *The Present Position (Non-official) of the Bishop's Curia of Mostar With Regard to the Events of Medjugorje*, in M O'Carroll, *Facts, Documents, Theology* (Veritas, Dublin, 1986) eg, page 102.

Applying the second positive criterion means looking more closely at the circumstances. What are the personal qualities of the six young people, of Mirjana, Ivan, Vicka, Jakov, Ivanka, and Marija? From having spoken with all of them, and — except for Mirjana — several times, my judgment is overwhelmingly positive regarding their psychological balance, their honesty, and their morals. They are model Catholics in every way. They love the Church and the sacraments. They have great, even exceptional, respect and reverence for Church authority, including that of Bishop Zanic. Their prayerfulness and their spiritual lives are outstanding. What is more, everyone I know shares my evaluation of these young people.

I have heard criticism. Once of Jakov: that he can be mischievous. And once of Mirjana: that she apparently tints her hair and uses curlers. Otherwise, nothing.

Is the theological doctrine and the spirituality of Medjugorje sound and free from error? In general, yes. And in particular, the weekly messages to the parish as well as Our Lady's message to all of peace, conversion, prayer, and penance and fasting, are clearly sound theologically and spiritually. Furthermore, the preaching of the Franciscan priests at the Masses, and their teaching when they explain Our Lady's messages, I find remarkably sound and ortho- dox and, moreover, practical and helpful spiritually.

What about Bishop Zanic's charge that some or at least one of Our Lady's messages, particularly to Vicka and Mirjana, show no respect for his authority and, in fact, undermine it by attacking it? I have studied this question, spoken to the people concerned — especially to the bishop and to Father Tomislav Vlasic — and I find no real evidence to substantiate this charge. True, Our Lady is said to have mildly criticised the bishop's impulsiveness in his treatment of two young Franciscan priests who were, as a result, suspended from the exercise of their priesthood and expelled from the Francis- can order. The bishop's impulsiveness in several matters is no secret. I find his conduct open to criticism regarding the two young priests. And I do not see why Our Lady could not have expressed the mild criticism she is said to have made. I simply do not see that as a problem.

Finally, as to the application of the last positive criterion to Medjugorje, regarding the healthy religious devotion and the spiritual fruits there, and regarding the spirit of prayer and the numerous conversions, no one contests the facts. Not even Bishop Zanic. Medjugorje has a deep spirit of prayer, and fervent and healthy religious devotion. I find no trace of unhealthy religious enthusiasm. And the great spiritual fruits of Medjugorje are admitted by everyone I know.

We can also apply the document's negative criteria to the events at Medjugorje. There is no obvious error about the main facts involved, about the central phenomena. I can find no doctrinal error attributed to God, to Our Lady, nor to any saint or angel.

And surely the young people and the Franciscans show no interest whatever in lucre. On the contrary. True, one finds greedy people in Medjugorje. One might run a restaurant with only financial gain from the pilgrims on his mind. Another might sell religious objects and trinkets at a roadside stand only to make some money. And the Yugoslavian government has made money through sponsoring tours to Medjugorje, especially from London, through its Yugoslav Tours agency. But these things are peripheral and do not touch the persons or facts or situation of Medjugorje.

● *Souvenirs for sale — but the young people and the Franciscans show no interest in money.*

I have no hint of grave immorality regarding any of the principal figures in the Medjugorje events: the six young people and the Franciscan priests and sisters. And I have seen no evidence of mental illness in either the young people or the Franciscans. Nor of psychopathic tendencies or psychoses.

How about collective hysteria or mass hallucination? I find no evidence of either among the pilgrims. Could the apparitions themselves be the result of collective hallucination or collective hysteria on the part of the six, now four, young persons? I do not see how. All the medical evidence so far goes against this hypothesis.

Applying the Vatican document's positive and negative criteria to Medjugorje gives a clear picture of lines of converging evidence toward a positive judgment as to the authenticity, the supernaturality, of those events.

The document from the Sacred Congregation for the Doctrine of the Faith also mentions possible intervention on the part of Church authorities. I have already made some comments on the way the local bishop has handled the situation. He has not at all followed the outlined action plan. Nor, in my opinion, has he tried to apply fairly the document's listed criteria for supernaturality. As far as I know, he has not referred the matter either to the Croatian-speaking bishops or to the Yugoslavian bishops' conference.

Given Bishop Zanic's slowness and, particularly, his lack of adherence to the document, and given the fact that the Sacred Congregation can intervene even without the bishop asking it to, it is not surprising that it has done so. What happens next remains to be seen.

• *Bishop Pavao Zanic: no
official statement.*

9. Darkness at Medjugorje (late January, 1986)

by Robert Faricy

January 24, Friday. I flew into Dubrovnik last night, stayed at the Hotel Petka, and caught the 9.25 bus for Caplina, where I took a taxi, and arrived as lunch began at the parish house here at Medjugorje. What has happened in my absence?

The most important news: Bishop Zanic has told Father Slavko Barbaric that he can no longer perform any ministry at Medjugorje: no celebrating Mass, no preaching, no leading the rosary or other devotions. This is, of course, a great blow to everyone here. And it means that the other priests — Ivan, Pero, Dobroslav, and the pastor Tomislav Pervan — will have a lot more to do.

Father Ivan announced after Mass, in Croatian, that Our Lady had told Vicka on January 6 that she would have no more apparitions until February 25, when they would begin again. And that, in the meantime, Our Lady had three things for her to do.

Tomislav Vlasic told me in the sacristy that Our Lady asked Vicka's consent to this plan. Vicka, he said, cried, but she did say 'Yes' to the plan. No one except Our Lady and Vicka knows the nature of the three things that Our Lady asked Vicka to do.

January 25, Saturday. Tonight, as on every Tuesday, Thursday, and Saturday night, the *velika grupa*, the 'big group' guided by Our Lady through Jelena and Marijana and with Tomislav Vlasic as chaplain, met after Mass in the large room in the basement of the parish house. The number has greatly diminished, from about 60 when the group began to about 30 now. Only three or four men come to the meetings, and many women and teenage girls.

At the same time, attendance at evening Mass and at the rosary before and after Mass has gone down considerably. Schools close during January, and this is a season of light work in the fields and at home. So people are relatively free to go to church in the evening. Yet comparatively few go. On weekday evenings, even with the pilgrims, the church remains not at all filled for weekday Mass, and only about half filled or less for the rosary. Most evenings Jakov does not come to Mass. Jelena and Marijana and the members of their prayer group do not stay for the glorious mysteries after Mass either. Only a few fervent souls and several pilgrims stay to the end.

What should I think about this apparent decline in fervour? That, like the rest of us, the people of Medjugorje can lose their initial fervour, can grow lax and become tepid, can get tired, can prefer to stay at home and perhaps watch television. The spiritual spring, summer, and autumn here in the parish were beautiful seasons. The winter of our spirituality comes inevitably. Not everyone makes it through the winter. The winter of spirituality tests us, purifies us, grounds us more in the Lord. If we remain faithful, then he can use us. Survival of the fittest.

January 27, Monday. Slavko just came into the dining room of the parish house, where I am studying Croatian, to tell me that the head of the secret police in Mostar telephoned him two minutes ago to tell him to report in tomorrow afternoon. Why?

Two years ago Slavko gave a four-day prayer seminar to young people here in Medjugorje. Early the second day the Mostar secret police picked him up and took him to Mostar for questioning about the seminar, about prayer, about meditation, about Our Lady. Thirteen hours straight of questioning. The third day of the seminar they took him in for 10 hours questioning. The fourth and last day, seven hours of interrogation. The apparent purpose: to disrupt the prayer seminar.*

*It is more than doubtful that the Bishop of Mostar notified the police about the seminar. Everyone I spoke to about the possibility of a connection between the bishop and the Mostar police categorically rejected the idea. This includes the Medjugorje Franciscan priests. It is true that the bishop's attitude has appeared to some non-Croatians as co-operative with the Yugoslavian government authorities (see: M O'Carroll, *Medjugorje: Facts, Documents, Theology*). But any such hypothesis is to be rejected.

Perhaps the secret police want to question Slavko now about his observance of the bishop's recent order not to do any ministry at Medjugorje. Slavko, of course, does not at all think for even a moment that the bishop has a direct link with the secret police.

January 29, Wednesday. Slavko cannot figure out what the police wanted him for. They kept him only a short time and did not seem to know what they were looking for. The head of the Mostar secret police asked Slavko: 'Who answered the phone when I telephoned for you? He does not speak Croatian well.' Slavko answered: 'It could have been anyone. Our house is quite international.' It was me.

Sister Lucy will come to Medjugorje in two weeks, on February 16. She will stay with Jozo Vasilj's family. I leave today.

10. Medjugorje winter (February, 1986)

by Lucy Rooney

February 15, Saturday. Rome, Leonardo Da Vinci Airport, 3.30 pm. Here I am in the departure lounge. Outside I can see the JAT aircraft on the tarmac, being serviced. The rain falls steadily. The few waiting passengers are bundled up against the cold, wet weather, but now they are overheated in the warm airport.

On board I am seated in row three, near the front of the plane. As I am thinking, 'If there were a first class, this would be it', I find that it is! The Croatian woman beside me, by signs and innuendoes, tells me that she is equally bewildered.

I asked for the Yugoslav daily newspapers, thinking that Jozo my host would like them — one rarely sees a newspaper in Medjugorje. (But when on my arrival I gave them to Marica his wife, she looked blankly for a moment, saying 'English?' Then she realised they were in Cyrillic script which only 10-year-old Ivana can read; it is compulsory in school, and detested.)

We come down through thick clouds, into Split. On the airport bus into the city, I am the only passenger. The driver is courteous. Every time I open my notebook to write, he switches on the light; the evening is very dark. The rain comes down more heavily. I struggle with my bag to the bus station, but there is no bus tonight for Citluk; so I struggle on to an hotel. As I leave the bus station, women pounce on me, saying: 'Sleeping?' They are landladies touting for customers. They may be fine, but they have a predatory manner. In fact, when I return next morning, there they are, and we all recognise each other.

February 16, Sunday. The church bells of Split begin ringing at 6 am.

I wonder if the neighbours complain? It is a grey morning, and by the time I leave the hotel the rain is falling again. I walk along the sea front to the bus, but the raw smell of the sea is almost too strong. Having bought my ticket, I have a little trouble finding the right bus, so I dump my bag on a bench and go off to ask a driver. Concerned that I might be late, he takes me by the arm and starts to run me to the 'Information' — I'm trying to stop him until I get my bag, but he tugs the harder! Finally we laugh, and off I go.

There are several young men on the bus; already they are half-drunk at 8 am. One of them, a pleasant, well-dressed boy, comes to speak to me in English. He asks the usual questions: Where do I come from? To where am I going? I don't mention Medjugorje. He is going, he says, to Sarajevo, adding in a mysterious voice, 'First, that is'. Being a little bothered at the thought of four hours in his company, I'm glad when, after some inebriated singing, they all fall asleep.

The bus drives south along the Adriatic coast, turns inland, and spirals up ever higher on the mountain road. The villages through which we pass seem deserted — a wet Sunday morning is a time for the fireside. After two hours we reach the snowline, but even here the snowfall has been light. From time to time we stop in a village and everyone alights to go into a café — except the sleeping youths, fortunately, for the men mostly drink plum brandy; the women take Turkish-style coffee.

So on, through this country of rocks, cream coloured, stained red by the earth, weathering to grey-black on the harsh mountains. This is the fifth day of rain, and from the height to which our bus has climbed, we look down on flooded fields in the river valley. The incessant 'canned music' on Yugoslav transport can spoil any journey. I wonder what the quality of 'public music' says about the quality of a society. The better parts of the programme sound like Islamic pop music; it could be, because Muslims are the majority in this area.

Later: I finally reached Jozo's house in Medjugorje, and, after drying out a little and taking tea with the family, I went down to the church. The first person I met, in the pouring rain, was the pastor, Tomislav Pervan. He gives one the best of welcomes. Then I found Father Pero Ljubicic serving in the little shop — no customers for religious objects today. Sister Janja was in the kitchen with Sister

Ana and Sister Danijela, who is replacing Sister Amalija for a few weeks, and, to my delight, Sister Josipa Kordic. Sister Josipa had to leave immediately, but will be back, maybe Wednesday, and has invited me to her sister's house in the village.

Within moments Sisters Janja and Ana set a hot meal before me, and while I ate, Sister Janja brought me up to date with events at Medjugorje. While we talked, the others came into the kitchen: Father Slavko, here for the day (he has *another* cold); Father Ivan, warmly smiling; Sister Ignacija, a quiet, strong woman. Two visitors came in: the Passionist Father Gianni Segreva with his sister Gabriella. They had come from Italy by bus.

The chief news was that yesterday, Saturday, February 15, Mirjana had a vision of Our Lady at her house here in Bijakovici. It lasted five or six minutes, and during it she saw again the first secret, as though in a film.

Jakov came into the kitchen, his hair in a quasi-punk cut, his belt a steel-studded affair. But I had the impression that he was in good shape. He is thin. Sister Janja introduced me — Jakov answered, 'O, I know her'. He managed to shake hands with more or less grace. Marija came in next — it does one good to meet her. She told us that about 20 people were trying to be admitted to the small room where Our Lady appears. 'It becomes impossible to breathe,' Marija said. Ivan arrived next. Vicka, I'm told, is praying much during this time when she is not seeing Our Lady. She is at daily Mass, sometimes the 7 am, sometimes the evening Mass either in the church or in the sacristy.

It was time for the rosary at five, so I went over to church. There were about 100 people there. Only a minority were foreigners: a dozen or so were Italians; a few were English-speaking, two of them Australians camping in their van, two others were from Alaska, one was from Thailand. A Yugoslav coach had brought a group of Croatian-speaking pilgrims. Father Jozo Zovko prayed in the back bench. One of the striking things about Medjugorje is the absorption with which people pray. By the time Mass began there was standing room only. The Mass lasted over an hour, then almost everyone remained for the Stations of the Cross. We finished at eight; then out into the rain to walk back home.

At supper, Anita Curtis, an Irish woman devoting her life to Medjugorje, translated parts of our book, *Medjugorje Unfolds* (published in the US as *Medjugorje Up Close*), for Jozo, Marica and grandmother Anda. They were embarrassed and pleased to be in print!

February 17, Monday. As I left the house this morning, Jozo was in the garden breaking ground for an extension to his house. He intends to build three more rooms and a bathroom. He will do the whole thing himself, as he built the existing house. It will take him 20 days, he says. He has all the materials ready; the only difficult part is the rock in the soil.

We had an English Mass at ten, said by Father Paschal Dillon, OMI. Milona von Habsburg was there.

After Mass I phoned Father Bob, in Rome, from the post office, as a trial run. There was a buzzing noise on the line, so communication was almost impossible. I was afraid to give any news of Mirjana's vision in case I was overheard.

Tonight there were only about 50 people in the church when the rosary began. More arrived for Mass, including three young Italian girls — religious of some sort, for though without veils, they wore ankle-length black coats over some kind of habit. One of them sang a solo *Magnificat* in a true voice.

February 18, Tuesday. All the telephones of Medjugorje have been out of order for 10 days. Only the one in the post office has been repaired. This at least gives the parish house some peace; people have been phoning from all over the world, as news is spread, inaccurately, about impending signs.

This morning I interviewed Father Pero Ljubicic with Sister Janja as interpreter. This is what he told me. He was present when Our Lady appeared to Mirjana on February 15. It was an exterior, not an interior vision, lasting five to six minutes. Our Lady prayed over Pero. I asked him if he would like to say how he felt, but he could not. Mirjana told him that Our Lady and she said an *Our Father* and a *Glory be* for strength for Pero and Mirjana. Then they said a second *Our Father* and *Glory be* for all the faithless, because things will be bad for them. A third was said for those who need our prayers. Mirjana then asked Our Lady if she could say a *Hail Mary*. 'Dear Madonna, can I pray to you the *Hail Mary*?'

I asked Pero about the document which Mirjana has received from Mary, and on which the secrets are written. He replied that before the first of the 10 secrets is to be revealed, Mirjana will give the document to him, and he will have it from then on. Within three days before the secret comes to pass all will know of it. He said that according to Mirjana there will be two warnings, ie, two of the secrets, before the sign appears on the hill Podbrdo.

This evening I was in Father Ivan's office-bedroom at five o'clock, for Our Lady's appearance. Over 20 of us squeezed in, standing so as to make more room. Ivan and Marija knelt just inside the door. Father Gianni led the rosary in Italian and in English. Marija introduced each mystery in Croatian. She and Ivan each said a decade, then other people took turns in their own language. Just before 5.45, Ivan and Marija stood facing the wall to wait for Our Lady. They prayed an *Our Father*, but suddenly stopped and fell to their knees. The vision lasted several minutes. At one point they prayed aloud an *Our Father* and a *Glory be*. People took flash photos. Some of those present were reverent and obviously moved. When Marija and Ivan came to themselves, making the sign of the cross, Ivan led us in saying the *Magnificat* and *Glory be*. We went immediately to church, Ivan waiting to lock the door after us. He and Marija went by the outside door into the sacristy to follow the Mass from there.

The church was full but not crowded. After Mass quite a number stayed for the prayers for the sick. By 8.30, when the third part of the rosary began, there remained only about 40 people — I counted at least 10 visitors, so that leaves around 30 parishioners. Their church attendance is undoubtedly falling off after four and a half years, except, it seems, on Sunday, on Thursday for the Holy Hour, and on Friday for the Way of the Cross. But at Jozo's house, family prayer has not lessened. The adults have given up meat and wine on four days a week during Lent. In winter here there is no fruit, the only fresh vegetable is cabbage, and very occasionally a little lettuce. So their diet is already restricted. Marija Pavlovic was offered coffee today at the rectory, but declined; she has given it up for Lent. Coffee and wine are the staple beverages; milk depends on the family cow.

February 19, Wednesday. There has been a Mass in English each morning said by Father Paschal Dillon, OMI. This is his last day here. His homilies are a delight. He knows the lives of all the saints and all the popes, and they crowd into every homily, stories and sayings apt for his purpose. He led us in making the Stations of the Cross after Mass. His comments on Our Lord's sufferings were almost more than I could bear.

Our good friend Father Svetozar Kraljevic joined us in making the Stations, and we talked together afterwards. He has read *Medjugorje Unfolds* and thought it very good. He says it is just what should be written at this time, showing the significance of events here. He added: 'It is a book that could only have been written by a friend.' He asked me how far news had spread of the bishop's latest accusation against Tomislav. He had heard that it had been in the press. I said I thought not. He agreed with Father Bob's counsel not to publish a defence.

There is a young woman here from the USA, Lynn Knapp. She is a friend and co-worker of Mother Angelica who has the TV network. Mother Angelica has her TV network ready to spread any message. Lynn phones Mother Angelica every day, speaking in a code they have arranged. But she says the post office have become suspicious, so now she goes to Citluk.

February 20, Thursday. The sun shone this morning, the first time it has been seen this week; but by noon the rain was back, with thunder and lightning. I went in to see Sister Janja, but she had gone to Ljubuski. Sister Ana gave me coffee, and while I drank it Fathers Slavko, Ivan and Dobroslav came in for theirs. Afterwards Slavko went to give an information session to four French-speaking pilgrims — two priests and a French Canadian man and wife. I have never seen fewer people here. A Yugoslav man from Grude told me that Our Lady had asked all six of the visionaries to be here today. These rumours are everywhere; it is impossible to know yet what is true.

While I was in the church towards midday, Jelena, Marijana, their friend Andrijana, and a fourth girl came in. They looked to see if the vision room was empty. As it was occupied, they knelt briefly in the front bench, then left, talking and giggling. They are very much country 13-year-olds. I feel that they would be lightweight if it were not for Our Lady's choice of them and this village.

Vicka was in church for the rosary and Mass this evening. The church was full, as Thursday is the parish special day, when Our

Lady gives the parishioners a message through Marija. This is the message for this week, February 20, 1986:

Dear children! The second message for Lent is: you must renew your prayer before the cross. Dear children, I offer you special graces, and Jesus gives you special gifts from the cross. Accept them and live them. Meditate on the passion of Jesus, and be united with Jesus in your lives.

After Mass there was a Holy Hour with exposition of the Blessed Sacrament. Father Jozo Zovko, the former pastor, who was imprisoned, led the prayers. Jelena Vasilj was among those who made readings and prayers. The reverence of the parishioners was impressive. The church remained full, and everyone knelt for the entire hour.

February 21, Friday. A slightly less wet day. The church was full for Mass this evening: I estimated about 700 people. As the visitors are just a handful, that means that of around 500 families of the parish, all could be represented. Most have young children, so both parents cannot come to church on the same evening. Almost everyone stayed for the Stations of the Cross — an hour long.

There have been government officials measuring the ground around the church — it is said, for shops as a deliberate attempt to commercialise Medjugorje. I asked if the ground were not the property of the parish. The answer was simple: the government has taken it.

February 22, Saturday. This morning at 6.45 I went up Krizevac, the hill of the cross. The sky was grey with impending rain. As I scrambled over the flint rocks I saw tiny crocus, purple and white, growing in every crevice beside and even on the path. I met no one. I had the whole morning world to myself; only the wind rustled in the thorn bushes and roosters crowed from the plain below.

Down at the church the weekend crowds are arriving. An English/Irish group has come with Jugotours; two coach-loads of Yugoslavs arrived during the morning. Towards the end of the evening Mass, the Italians descended on Medjugorje.

Before Mass, as the parish house was locked, I went down to the public toilets — those three holes in the ground, with the river flowing below. It was a mistake! Although some heroic person cleans them, the smell is bad. I had to sit outside the church all during Mass, trying to recover. Then I heard the good news that finally the government has seen the light (or smelled the smell!) and given permission: toilets can be built, work to begin in April.

February 23, Sunday. Four babies were baptised at the 8.30 Mass this morning. They, their parents and sponsors were in the sanctuary for the whole Mass, which lasted over an hour. But there was not even a whimper from the babies. Their baptism took place after the Creed.

The English group were due to have Mass in the chapel of the apparitions at 9.30, but it was 9.45 before we could begin. We were far too many for the small room; half of us were standing. Finally one man collapsed.

Today I climbed the hill Podbrdo to the site of the first apparitions. There is quite a forest of crosses there now, so it is not easy to distinguish the actual places where Our Lady stood. As I passed Ivan's house I saw him patiently, doggedly, speaking to the Italian pilgrims while his friends laughed in the background. Ivan finds the attention to which he is subjected almost unbearable.

Bijakovici village is more rural than Medjugorje. Many of the houses keep pigs, and the older people pasture goats and sheep on the hillside.

We had a birthday party at Jozo's this afternoon — Marija Vasilj Tunin is now three years old! She accepted her gifts with grace, shaking hands with, then kissing, each guest. Her mother had baked a special cake. The children's aunt, Sister Innocenza, OFM, Baba-Anda's sister, spent the night here. At the party she told us, through Jozo, how the cross on Mount Krizevac was built in 1933. The men and women of the parish carried up the concrete and other materials on their backs or on donkeys. The children, of whom Sister Innocenza was one, carried whatever they could. Jozo says a photograph was taken — but only of the men! The priest who had the idea of building the cross was a man of the Holy Spirit, Jozo said; the cross was in God's plan. He was subsequently shot in 1945 along with so many other men and Franciscan priests of this area of Bosnia-Hercegovina. Jozo says that when he was a child, he and Anda his mother often did not have enough of even bread to eat. He was 17 years old before he saw a sweet. People now, we were told, still cannot bear to eat carob bread, because they had to live on it in those days.

Father Slavko left today for his speaking tour. Milona von Habsburg went with him as interpreter.

February 24, Monday. I telephoned Father Bob this morning, from the Medjugorje post office — the only phone in the district which functions. As soon as I rang off, the girl clerk began dialling. I wondered. Bob says Italy is full of rumours that Medjugorje is to be closed down, that the police are moving in. Certainly the Italians are moving in! I passed two cars of important-looking clergy: they beamed at me while speeding by, splashing me with a tidal wave of muddy water!

I have never known such an atmosphere of oppression at Medjugorje. I took a bus to Mostar today to buy my return ticket to Rome. It was the same there. Crowds of men stand idle on the street corners. At first one wonders what is wrong: why is there a crowd? Then one realises. A depressed and depressing society, it is relieved by the people, by their small acts of kindness — the kindly, courteous people who direct one, the bus ticket men who, if one does not have enough small change, take what one has. Do they make it up from their own pockets?

During Mass this evening Sister Janja whispered to me that we, three American women and I, who are staying with Jozo, could go up Mount Krizevac where Our Lady will appear to Ivan, Vicka and Marija as they and their prayer group meet, as they do each Monday and Friday. We were to be at the foot of the mountain at 8.30 pm.

Marica gave us an early supper and hospitably welcomed two pilgrims from England: Bridie and her Irish husband Tony Gallagher. They are involved in anti-abortion work in London. England, they said, is the abortion capital of the world. Recently Bridie herself saw Our Lady as she was coming down from Podbrdo, as did the man who was with her. This evening, as their house was in quite the opposite direction from Krizevac, they came to wait for us at Jozo's.

When we arrived at the meeting point we found half of the Italian contingent already there. So Bridie, Tony and I went up ahead. Climbing that rocky path in the dark is difficult enough, without doing it in a bunch. I could have gone up like a mountain goat, but as it was dark, and we had been warned not to use torches for fear of the police, I waited to show the way to the less agile Bridie. At times I feared I had lost the path myself; but all was well. A fierce, rain-filled wind was blowing up there on the ridge. I went round behind the cross — and there was a surprise: John McMahon, an old friend of ours and of Medjugorje!

Almost everyone who turns up here finds that they either have met before, or have friends in common, or once lived in the same street, or are just about to move to the same parish. I couldn't sort out all the cross-currents this evening — a whirl of people.

John and I had a reunion up there while we waited for the main group who were singing and praying their way from station to station on the Way of the Cross. Afterwards, the American women, Grace and Margie, told us how youngsters had helped and urged them on in the climb.

Of those who see Our Lady, only Ivan was present this evening. A group of Italian pilgrims took Marija and Vicka with them in their bus to visit Father Jozo Zovko. They were to have Mass there, and promised to return Marija and Vicka to Medjugorje by 7 pm. But they detained them so long that they were too late to come to Mount Krizevac, and so missed their meeting with Our Lady.

After we had prayed for a while at the foot of the great cross, there was a long silence during which Ivan saw and spoke with the

• *Ivan Dragicevic —*
seeing and speaking with
the Blessed Mother.

Blessed Mother. But most of the pilgrims stood up, crowding round him. Between them and the darkness I could not see even who of the visionaries was there. I was impressed by those people who, on the fringes of the crowd, absorbed themselves in prayer, bowed down to the ground, not desiring to see the visionaries or anything spectacular.

At the end, Ivan described what he had seen. Again I could not hear, but a translation in English finally reached us: Our Lady had come with five angels; she was very happy that we were there, blessed us, and prayed for us for a long time; she thanked us for our prayer and sacrifices this evening, and said that they had helped her with a plan she has today; she left in light.

Then began a nightmare descent of the mountain. All those feet passing over the rocks had coated them with mud. I don't know how some people made it at all. The path seemed interminable. It was almost midnight when we reached the road. Bridie, Tony and their group still had a long walk to their lodgings — and they were leaving for the airport at 2 am! It was quite an evening.

February 25, Tuesday. There is a vigorous north-west wind this morning and a light snowfall. I called into the rectory kitchen to visit Sister Janja. Father Ivan came in and greeted me. Sister Janja spoke to him briefly while I was washing my coffee cup. When he had gone, Janja said to me: 'I asked Father Ivan (who has the care of the visionaries) if you could be in the vision room this evening.' Today is February 25 — the day on which Vicka's visions of Our Lady recommence. She has not seen the Blessed Mother since January 6. During that time she has had three things to do for Our Lady. These she has not made known. Sister Janja told me to come early, and she would hide me in the kitchen. Later I met Father Tomislav Pervan, the pastor, who called out to me: 'Lucy — be sure to be up at the house early.' It's a great privilege.

As I walked down to church in the afternoon it occurred to me that I should wash the caked mud from my wellington boots. I stopped on the road to inspect them — knowing they were muddy to the knees. And there I found, they had been washed! I discovered later that Marica and the children, Ivana, Angelina and Mate, had washed their own and everyone else's boots. That is typical of the extra love of adults and children here.

At 4 pm, Father Tomislav Vlasic gave an information session and a relection on Our Lady's messages, to about 200 Italian pilgrims. At 4.30 I left them and went across to the rectory. The wind was icy. I was glad to be in the kitchen, warmed by a wood and charcoal stove. Sister Janja's 20-year-old niece was there, named for her, and very like her. Presently Ivan arrived. I think part of his reserve is diffidence; he is always happy to escape fuss. Jakov had classes at school, so would see Our Lady in his own home later in the evening. Vicka came in and shook hands with a grip that left one's fingers tingling. Then Marija arrived, winked at me, greeted the others and went straight over to help in cutting up cabbages for the community supper. Father Tomislav Vlasic came in — gentle and courteous. Vicka conveyed to him by a glance how pent up she was with joy. He asked me how Father Bob was, and what news there was from Rome. I told him of the rumours. He threw up his hands, and an animated conversation went on in Croatian.

Then we were called, as it was five o'clock. Sister Janja told me to stick with Marija. So we went into the small room. Fewer people than usual were allowed in. Father Tomislav Pervan had set up a camera on a tripod. Another man had a small video camera. There were several priests, a young boy in a wheelchair and a few men and women. We knelt just inside the door — Marija, Sister Janja, Ivan and myself, with Vicka in front. Sister Janja introduced each mystery of the rosary: the joyful and sorrowful mysteries. The three young people took it in turns to lead a decade, then others took turns — one in Italian. Sister Janja called on Father Denis O'Sullivan, an Irish priest who works in New York. He led a decade in Irish.

Just after the fourth sorrowful mystery, Ivan, Vicka and Marija moved to the front of the group. They had hardly begun to pray the *Our Father* when they fell to their knees. According to Professor Joyeux, they react together in one-fifth of a second. He says such syncronisation is impossible to explain. Their explanation is that they react to the light which comes before Our Lady appears. I could not see Vicka's face — just Marija — but it did not seem important. One is in the immediate presence of Our Lady, and the visionaries cease to matter. The things one wants to ask cease to matter. It seemed to me that to pray out of love, not out of one's needs, was the thing. Love would cure everything.

Vicka's exclamation, '*Ode*' ('She's gone') startled us. I could see that Marija had difficulty in returning to herself. Ivan began the *Magnificat*. Then we all stood — Marija and Ivan full of joy. As for Vicka, Sister Janja said: 'She is so happy, I could cry.'

Maybe it is the change in the weather, but I felt the lifting of the atmosphere over Medjugorje this evening, and when we were in the middle of supper, the telephone system came to life! Medjugorje is no longer cut off from outside.

Marica and her friends had intended to make the Way of the Cross up Mount Krizevac at 8.30 pm, but the freezing wind was so strong that they did not go. Snow would not have deterred them, but the wind might be dangerous up there.

February 26, Wednesday. I set off at 6.40 this morning. The north wind blows right through one's chest, and the flooded parts of the road are frozen over. After stopping briefly in church, I walked along by the river to the post office, which opens at seven; I wanted to telephone to Father Bob in Rome. The primary-school children were straggling along to school. Some must walk for well over 30 minutes. It is as well they do not go to school until they are seven years old. This morning they were delighting in cracking the ice on the puddles.

At the post office I had to wait while the clerk made his calls. I got through to Rome without trouble, but as soon as I said 'All is quiet here', the line went dead. At least I had given the essential message.

Vicka spoke to Father Ivan privately last evening, but so far nothing is known of her encounter with Our Lady.

I knelt at the back of the church this evening; it was not quite full, a very cold evening. Marijana, Andrijana and Jelena came in and waited for confession.

Ivan joins the congregation for Mass most evenings instead of following it from the sacristy as he used to do. At the consecration, Jakov came in with his school satchel over his shoulder. He joined his aunt and uncle and their two small girls. He will see Our Lady later in the evening, at home.

Everything comes full-circle in Medjugorje. As I was kneeling in church this evening, Sister Melanija, who used to be part of the parish staff, came in. I greeted her and told her I was going home tomorrow via Dubrovnik. It was just the ride she needed. We went over to the house to arrange it with Sister Janja. On the way I met Father Michael O'Carroll, the Irish Marian scholar.

February 27, Thursday. This morning the temperature is below freezing, but the wind is less keen. I went to the community Mass at 7am, celebrated by Father Pero, assisted by Tomislav Pervan, Dobroslav and Ivan. This must be a tranquil moment each day for the four priests and four sisters.

Back at Jozo's for breakfast: Ivana, the little sister of Jelena Vasilj, came in to call for Angelina. Ivana has an exceptional look of peace on her face — an interesting child. She is Marica's niece.

Jozo and I set off for Dubrovnik airport, first calling in at the rectory to pick up Sister Melanija. Melanija is studying nursing in Dubrovnik, but visits Medjugorje whenever she can. In the kitchen, Sister Janja tells me she had only an hour to talk to 'this little one', Melanija. Janja packed some good things for the family with whom Melanija lodges. She put them in a plastic bag — a relic of some pilgrim, for it had 'Merry Christmas' all over it, in English.

Janja told me a little about Vicka's meeting with Our Blessed Lady last Tuesday evening after 50 days of not seeing her. She said that Marija, teasing, said: 'You should have seen the Madonna greeting Vicka — the whole apparition was about that!' Father Ivan had asked Vicka about her obviously improved health, and the rumours that she had been cured of the brain cyst. Vicka said, No, these rumours were not true. Janja asked Vicka what she could say to people who asked about her time without Our Lady, and now her seeing her again. Vicka said her health and her suffering were a very, very, small part of the project she had with the Blessed Mother during those days.

We said Goodbye and set off for the three-hour drive. As we neared the coast, the first signs of spring became apparent: blossom on the almond trees; wild narcissi, yellow and orange, growing among the black stumps of the burnt-out trees. So many fires devastated these hillsides last summer that arson was suspected. We stopped briefly at the ancient Franciscan monastery at Slano. Sister Melanija gathered for me a little bunch of wild violets from the tiny cloister garden. Their scent filled the car. We drove down into Dubrovnik city, along the wharf where timber was being loaded, and pleasure yachts bobbed alongside lobster boats.

Our flight was above a snow-field of clouds, with just the peaks of the Italian Apennines thrusting through to the blue sky. As we came down to Fiumicino Airport, there was a perfect panorama of Rome — the train station, the Coloseum, Piazza Venezia and Saint Peter's, with the River Tiber snaking to the sea.

• *Sister Lucy Rooney at Medjugorje. 'Almost everyone who turns up here finds that they either have met before, or have friends in common...'*

Epilogue

by Robert Faricy

September 25, 1986. Sister Lucy and I arrived last night by taxi from the airport. We went directly to the house where Jakov Colo lives with his aunt and uncle, in a cluster of houses down a dirt and rock road in Bijakovici. Jakov was in bed. His uncle found a room for Sister Lucy across the road. I left my bag with her and walked in the still black night to the church. Entering by the side door, I went up a circular stairway to the balcony, where I found a thick blanket, laid it on the floor, and went to sleep.

Lots of changes here. Sister Hyacinthe, who learned English working in Chicago, has replaced Sister Janja as superior of the sisters — five now instead of four, with only Sister Ana remaining from last winter. Sister Janja has become vice-provincial of her province, and visits Medjugorje often, especially on weekends. A new young priest has come: Father Nicola Vucic.

The Franciscans have built a new parish office and religious goods store, with rooms on the upper floor for three of the sisters. Toilets for men and women have replaced the notorious three holes. Souvenir shops, trinket stands, food stalls, and coffee and soft-drink bars proliferate. I found only one of these operated by a Catholic. Gypsies and Serbs and atheists from Mostar, Dubrovnik, and other places, have received permits from the government for commercial activity on the government land around the church and parish house. No local person does any commercial activity there; they know the Franciscans disapprove.

Much activity. Father Ivan works with a crew making wine. Sister Hyacinthe is making *sarma*. The other priests and sisters are busy today with the many pilgrims.

In the basement of the parish house, two Italian artists have stripped the accumulated layers of paint from Our Lady's statue that stood for so many years in the original apparitions room in the church. Yesterday, Anita Curtis came to the basement just as the Italians came to the original layer of paint and decoration. The statue came from Austria many years ago; it was decorated there. But over Our Lady's right breast the Croatian word for 'peace', *mir*, is painted in gold letters! Marija, when she saw it, broke into praise and said 'Alleluia' over and over.

Some things stay the same. The phone works only for local calls; all other outgoing calls receive a busy signal. And incoming long distance calls from Rome are blocked, although the parish house can be telephoned from other places.

Ivan is doing his required military service in Ljubljana; he should come home in June, 1987. They say the army intends to send him soon for language study, perhaps English. He sees Our Lady only when he is away from the base, on pass or on furlough. But he has contact of some kind with her in his personal prayer.

Jakov still attends secondary school in Citluk. Marija, always smiling and gracious, spends time with the pilgrims, helps the priests in the sacristy before and after Mass, and by her presence gives witness to God's love for each of us.

Vicka's health remains poor, but today we saw her talking to pilgrims near the church. January 6, 1986, Our Lady asked Vicka to make special sacrifices. This request seems somehow connected with the fact that Vicka has long stretches of time in which she has no apparitions. Beginning January 6, 1986, she did not see Our Lady for 50 days. On April 22, Our Lady revealed the ninth secret to Vicka. Then, starting April 23, Vicka had no apparitions for 40 days. The third period of time with no apparitions began on August 24, and will end on October 20. This is all quite mysterious, and Vicka does not explain it.

So all four — Vicka, Marija, Ivan, Jakov — now have nine of the 10 secrets. The first two will be warnings; the third will be a permanent sign on Podbrdo, the hill of the first apparitions. Some of the secrets foretell good things. But the last three, it seems, tell of terrible events. Vicka wept greatly at the ninth secret.

Mirjana frequently comes to Medjugorje for a few days' holiday. She sees Our Lady occasionally. A week ago, Mirjana and Vicka make a short retreat in a Franciscan parish about 40 miles from here.

Ivanka will see Our Lady every year on June 25, the anniversary of the first apparition in 1981. Last June 25, Our Lady spoke to Ivanka for 14 minutes about the 10 secrets and about Ivanka's personal life. And she encouraged Ivanka to pray much and to encourage others to pray much.

Jelena and Marijana have begun secondary school in Mostar. The Blessed Virgin continues to give them prophecies for two of the Medjugorje prayer groups. In recent months, she has repeatedly stressed the importance of personal prayer.

In the afternoon, I visit Father Ivan in his office. We talk about recent happenings here. Sometimes he refers to a log-book in which he keeps a daily record of what Our Lady does here at Medjugorje. Father Ivan tells me that, in spite of rumours to the contrary, the official diocesan commission (dissolved on May 2, 1986, and of which he was a member) made no report. Each member wrote a personal report to Bishop Zanic, and these were forwarded to the Vatican. And the bishop asked for a secret vote as to the authenticity of the apparitions. No one except the bishop knows the results of that vote.

In the evening, Sister Lucy and I go to Father Slavko's room to pray the rosary and watch Jakov and Marija have their daily visit from Our Lady. Our Lady gives Marija the Thursday night message for the parish, and for all of us:

Dear children! Through your own peace, I am calling you to help others to see and to start searching for peace. You are, dear children, at peace, and you cannot comprehend absence of peace. Therefore I am calling you, so that through your prayer and your life you help to destroy everything evil in people, and uncover the deceptions that Satan uses. Pray for truth to prevail in every heart. Thank you for your response to my call.

September 26, 1986. In the morning, I come down from the church balcony to meet Sister Lucy and to head for Dubrovnik. The sun comes up over the parish house like a bright Host.

Appendix: Our Lady's messages to the parish and the world

by Lucy Rooney

Early in 1984 Our Lady asked, through Jelena Vasilj, that the people of the Medjugorje parish should gather once a week in prayer. At their first meeting, at Mass on March 1, 1984, the Blessed Mother gave them a message through Marija Pavlovic. She said 'I have chosen this parish in a special way, and I wish to lead it.' The messages which have followed each Thursday have been a programme of formation beginning with the second meeting's basic 'start converting yourselves', followed by the corollary (which characterises authentic spirituality: a turning out to share the gifts and fruits of the encounter with the Lord): 'In that way, all who come here will be able to convert.'

It is fascinating to trace the themes of this programme, and how they are related to the unfolding year of the Church's liturgy and the daily life of a mainly small-scale farming society in a late twentieth-century milieu, within an often repressive socio-political system.

The teaching methods — encouragement, repetition, disappointment, loving severity, consolation, strengthening, rejoicing — are all those a mother would employ. There is no softness here, but great love and touching courtesy. And there is a chilling reality — a facing up with urgency to the realities which are no less threatening for being often denied: 'Love those from whom evil comes to you' (November 7, 1985); 'Enter the battle against Satan' (August 8, 1985). There is equally a reminder of the true but unseen dimension in which we live: 'You are occupied with material things; I am inviting you to pray for the gifts of the Holy Spirit' (April 17, 1986);

'I am calling you to holiness; without holiness you cannot live' (July 10, 1986).

Our Lady's training programme is for each of us. She told the people: 'You [the parish] must receive my messages first, and then the others' (February 6, 1985). This is how she calls us, each one: 'Dear children, listen, and live the Mother's call, because I am calling you only out of love so that I may keep you' (January 16, 1986).

The messages

March 1, 1984. 'Dear children! I have chosen this parish in a special way and I wish to lead it. I am guarding it in love and I wish everyone to be mine. Thank you for your response this evening. I wish that you will always be in greater numbers with me and my Son. Every Thursday I will speak a special message to you.'

March 8, 1984. 'Dear children! In this parish start converting yourselves. In that way all those who come here will be able to convert. Thank you for your response to my call.'

March 15, 1984. 'This evening, dear children, in a special way I am grateful to you for being here. Adore continually the Most Holy Sacrament. I am always present when the faithful are in adoration. Special graces are then being received.' This day, like every Thursday evening, the faithful were worshipping the Most Holy Sacrament, but this evening it was noticed that many men remained in the church for adoration, although they had worked hard in the fields.

March 22, 1984. 'Dear children! This evening I am asking you in a special way during this Lent to honour the wounds of my Son, which He received from the sins of this parish. Unite with my prayers for this parish so that His sufferings may become bearable. Thank you for your response to my call. Make an effort to come in greater numbers.'

March 29, 1984. 'Dear children! This evening in a special way I am asking for your perseverance in trials. Ponder how the Almighty is still suffering because of your sins. So when sufferings come, offer them as your sacrifice to God. Thank you for your response to my call.'

April 5, 1984. 'Dear children! This evening I am especially asking you to venerate the Heart of my Son Jesus. Make atonement for the wounds inflicted to the Heart of my Son. That Heart has been offended with all sorts of sin. Thank you for coming this evening.'

April 12, 1984. 'Dear children! This evening I ask you to stop slandering and pray for the unity of the parish, for my Son and I have a special plan with this parish. Thank you for your response to my call.'

April 19, 1984. 'Dear children! Sympathise with me. Pray, pray, pray.'

April 26, 1984. 'Although this was Thursday Our Lady gave me no message.' Therefore Marija came to the conclusion that probably Our Lady was going to give the Thursday messages only during Lent. However, on April 30 she asked Our Lady: 'Dear Our Lady, why have you not given me the message for the parish on Thursday?' Our Lady replied: 'Even though I have a special message for the parish to awaken the faith of every believer, I do not wish to force anyone to do anything he doesn't feel or doesn't want. Only a very small number has accepted the messages on Thursday. At the beginning there were more, but now it seems as if it has become something ordinary to them. And some have been asking recently for the message only out of curiosity, and not out of faith and devotion to my Son and me.'

May 10, 1984. Many believers were struck by the last message of Our Lady. Many thought that Our Lady was not going to give messages for the parish anymore. But this evening she said this: 'I am still speaking to you and I intend to continue. Just listen to my instructions.'

May 17, 1984. 'Dear children! Today I am very happy because there are many who desire to devote themselves to me. I thank you. You have not made a mistake. My Son Jesus Christ wishes to bestow on you special graces through me. My Son is happy because of your dedication. Thank you for your response to my call.'

May 24, 1984. 'Dear children! I have told you already that I have chosen you in a special way, the way you are, I, the Mother, love you all. And in any moment when it is difficult for you, don't be afraid. I love you all, even when you are far away from me and my Son. I ask you not to allow my heart to cry with tears of blood because of the souls who are being lost in sin. Therefore, dear children, pray, pray, pray. Thank you for your response to my call.'

May 31, 1984. This was the Feast of the Ascension. There were many people from abroad. Our lady did not give any message. She said to Marija that she would give the message on Saturday, to be announced to the people on Sunday.

June 2, 1984. This was Saturday, and the novena of Pentecost. 'Dear children! This evening I wish to say: In the days of this novena, pray for the outpouring of the Holy Spirit upon all of your families and your parish. Pray, and you shall not regret it. God shall give you the gifts and you shall glorify Him for them until the end of your life. Thank you for your response to my call.'

June 9, 1984. Last Thursday again Our Lady did not give any messages for the parish. She promised she would give it this evening. The message is: 'Dear children! Tomorrow night pray for the Spirit of truth, especially you from the parish. The Spirit of truth is necessary for you in order to convey the messages just as I give them to you, not adding anything or taking anything away. Pray that the Holy Spirit inspires you with the Spirit of prayer, that you pray more. I as your Mother say that you pray little. Thank you for your response to my call.'

June 14, 1984. No special message was given.

June 21, 1984. 'Pray, pray, pray! Thank you for your response to my call.'

June 28, 1984. No special message was given.

July 5, 1984. 'Dear children! Today I wish to tell you: Always pray before your work and end your work with prayer. If you do that, God will bless you and your work. These days you have been praying too little and working too much. Pray therefore. In prayer you will find rest. Thank you for your response to my call.'

July 12, 1984. 'Dear children! These days Satan is trying to thwart all my plans. Pray that his plan may not be fulfilled. I will pray to my Son Jesus that He will give you the grace to experience His victory in Satan's temptations. Thank you for your response to my call.'

July 19, 1984. 'Dear children! These days you have been experiencing how Satan is working. I am always with you and do not be afraid of temptations. God is always watching over you. I have given myself up to you and I sympathise with you even in the smallest temptation. Thank you for your response to my call.'

July 26, 1984. 'Dear children! Today also I would like to call you to persistent prayer and penance. Especially let the young people of this parish be more active in their prayer. Thank you for your response to my call.'

August 2, 1984. 'Dear children! Today I am happy and I thank you for your prayers. Pray more these days for the conversion of sinners. Thank you for your response to my call.'

August 11, 1984. Our Lady did not give a message last Thursday. This is what she said to Marija this evening: 'Dear children! Pray, because Satan is continually trying to thwart my plans. Pray with your heart and in prayer give yourselves to Jesus.'

August 14, 1984. This apparition was unexpected. Ivan was praying in his house. After that he started getting ready for going to church for the evening service. Unexpectedly Our Lady appeared to him and asked him to relate this message to the people: 'I ask the people to pray with me these days. Pray all the more. Fast strictly on Wednesday and Friday; pray every day at least one rosary: joyful, sorrowful and glorious mysteries.' Our Lady asked the people to accept this message with a firm will. She asked this in a special way from the parishioners and believers of the surrounding places.

August 16, 1984. 'Dear children! I beg all of you, especially those from this parish, to live my messages and relate them with whomever you meet. Thank you for your response to my call.'

August 23, 1984. 'Pray, pray, pray!' Marija informed us that Our Lady had asked the people, especially the young, to keep order in the church during Mass.

August 30, 1984. 'Dear children! The cross was in God's plan when you built it. Especially these days go on the hill and pray at the foot of the cross. I need your prayers. Thank you for your response to my call.'

September 6, 1984. 'Dear children! Without prayer there is no peace. Therefore I say to you dear children, pray at the foot of the cross for peace. Thank you for your response to my call.'

September 13, 1984. 'Dear children! I continually need your prayer. You wonder what all these prayers are for. Turn around, dear children, and you will see how much ground sin has gained in this world. Therefore, pray that Jesus conquers. Thank you for your response to my call.'

September 20, 1984. 'Dear children! Today I ask you to start fasting from your heart. There are many people who fast but only because everyone is fasting. It has become a custom which no one wants to stop. I ask the parish to fast out of gratitude to God for allowing me to remain this long in the parish. Dear children, fast and pray with your heart. Thank you for your response to my call.'

September 27, 1984. 'Dear children! Your prayer has helped my plans to be fulfilled. Pray continually for their complete fulfilment. I beg the families of the parish to pray the family rosary. Thank you for your response to my call.'

October 4, 1984. 'Dear children! Today I would like to tell you that your prayers delight me, but there are those in the parish who do not pray and my heart is sad. Pray therefore that I may bring all your sacrifices and prayers to the Lord. Thank you for your response to my call.'

October 8, 1984. This message was given to the parish through Jakov in his home. He did not go to the church on that day because he was unwell. This is the message: 'Dear children! Let all the prayers you say in your homes in the evening be for the conversion of sinners, because the world is in great sin. Pray the rosary every evening.'

October 11, 1984. 'Dear children! Thank you for the offering of all your pains to God, even now when He is testing you through the fruits which you are reaping. Realise, dear children, that He loves you and for that reason He tests you. Always present your burdens to God and do not worry. Thank you for your response to my call.' The testing was a long rain in the middle of the reaping season which caused great damage to the harvest.

October 18, 1984. 'Dear children! Today I ask you to read the Bible in your homes every day and let it be in a visible place there, so that it always encourages you to read and pray. Thank you for your response to my call.'

October 25, 1984. 'Dear children! Pray during this month. God gave this month to me. I give it to you. Pray and ask for the graces of God. I will pray that He gives them to you. Thank you for your response to my call.'

November 1, 1984. 'Dear children! Today I call you to renewal of family prayer in your homes. The field work is over. Now let all of you be devoted to prayer. Let prayer take the first place in your families. Thank you for your response to my call.'

November 8, 1984. 'Dear children! You are not aware of the messages which God is sending to you through me. He is giving you great graces and you are not grasping them. Pray to the Holy Spirit for enlightenment. If you only knew the greatness of the graces God was giving you, you would pray without ceasing. Thank you for your response to my call.'

November 15, 1984. 'You are a chosen people and God gave you great graces. You are not aware of every message I am giving you. Now I only wish to say: Pray, pray, pray. I do not know what else to tell you because I love you and wish that in prayer you come to know my love and the love of God. Thank you for your response to my call.'

November 22, 1984. 'Dear children! These days live all the main messages and continue to root them into your hearts this week. Thank you for your response to my call.' 'This week' means the end of one liturgical season and the beginning of Advent.

November 29, 1984. 'Dear children! You do not know how to love and you do not know how to listen with love to the words I am giving you. Be aware, my beloved, that I am your Mother and that I have to come to the earth to teach you how to listen out of love, how to pray out of love, and not out of compulsion of the cross you are carrying. Through the cross God is being glorified in every man. Thank you for your response to my call.'

December 6, 1984. 'Dear children! These days I am calling you to family prayer. In God's name many times I have been giving you messages but you did not listen. This Christmas will be unforgettable for you only if you accept the messages I am giving you. Dear children, do not allow that day of joy to be a day of greatest sorrow for me. Thank you for your response to my call.'

December 13, 1984. 'Dear children! You know that the day of joy is coming near, but without love you will attain nothing. Therefore first of all start loving your family, everyone in the parish, and then you will be able to love and accept all those who are coming here. Let this week be the week of learning to love. Thank you for your response to my call.'

December 20, 1984. 'Today I am asking you to do something practical for Jesus Christ. On the day of joy I wish that every family of the parish brings a flower as a sign of abandonment to Jesus. I wish that every member of the family has one flower next to the crib so that Jesus can come and see your devotion to Him. Thank you for your response to my call.'

December 27, 1984. 'Dear children! This Christmas Satan wanted in a special way to thwart God's plans. You, dear children, have discerned Satan even on Christmas day. But in your hearts God has conquered. Let your hearts be continually joyful.'

January 3, 1985. 'Dear children! These days the Lord has granted you many graces. Let this week be a week of thanksgiving for all the graces God has granted you. Thank you for your response to my call.'

January 10, 1985. 'Dear children! Today I want to thank you for all your sacrifices. Especially I thank those who have become dear to my heart and come here gladly. There are many parishioners who are not listening to the messages. But because of those who are in a special way close to my heart, because of them, I give messages to the parish. And I will continue giving them for I love you and wish you to spread them by your hearts. Thank you for your response to my call.'

January 17, 1985. 'In these days Satan is fighting deviously against this parish, and you, dear children, are asleep in prayer, and only some are going to Mass. Persevere in these days of temptation. Thank you for your response to my call.'

January 24, 1985. 'Dear children! These days you have savoured the sweetness of God through renewal in your parish. Satan is working even more violently to take away the joy from each of you. Through prayer you can totally disarm him and ensure your happiness. Thank you for your response to my call.'

January 31, 1985. 'Dear children! Today I wish to tell you to open your hearts to God like flowers in spring yearning for the sun. I am your Mother and I always want you to be closer to the Father and that He will always give abundant gifts to your hearts. Thank you for your response to my call.'

February 7, 1985. 'Dear children! Satan is manifesting himself in this parish in a particular way these days. Pray, dear children, that God's plan is carried out, and that every work of Satan is turned to the glory of God. I have remained this long to help you in your trials. Thank you for your response to my call.'

February 14, 1985. 'Dear children! Today is the day when I give you the message for the parish, but the whole parish is not accepting the messages and does not live them. I am sad, and I wish you, dear children, to listen to me and to live my messages. Every family must pray family prayer and read the Bible. Thank you for your response to my call.'

February 21, 1985. 'Dear children! From day to day I have been appealing to you for renewal and prayer in the parish. But you are not accepting. Today I am appealing to you for the last time. This is the season of Lent, and you as a parish in Lent can be moved for the sake of love to my call. If you do not do that, I do not wish to give you my messages. God has permitted me. Thank you for your response to my call.'

February 28, 1985. 'Dear children! Today I call you to live the Word this week: I LOVE GOD! Dear children, with love you will achieve everything, and even what you think is impossible. God wants this parish to belong to Him completely. And I want that too. Thank you for your response to my call.'

March 7, 1985. 'Dear children! Today I invite you to renew prayer in your families. Dear children, encourage the very young to pray and to go to Holy Mass. Thank you for your response to my call.'

March 14, 1985. 'Dear children! In your life you have all experienced light and darkness. God gave to each person knowledge of good and evil. I am calling you to the light, which you have to carry to all people who are in darkness. From day to day people who are in darkness come to your homes. Give them, dear children, the Light. Thank you for your response to my call.'

March 21, 1985. 'Dear children! I want to give you the messages, and therefore today also I call you to live and to accept my messages. Dear children, I love you and in a special way I have chosen this parish, which is more dear to me than others where I have gladly been when the Almighty sent me. Therefore I call you: Accept me, dear children, for your wellbeing. Follow the messages. Thank you for your response to my call.'

March 24, 1985. 'Dear children! Today I wish to call you to confession, even if you had confession a few days ago. I wish you to experience my Feast Day within yourselves. You cannot, unless you give yourselves to God completely. And so I am calling you to reconciliation with God. Thank you for your response to my call.'

March 28, 1985. 'Dear children! Today I want to call you. Pray, pray, pray! In prayer you will come to know the greatest joy, and the way out of every situation that has no way out. And I thank all of you who have rekindled prayer in your families. Thank you for your response to my call.'

April 4, 1985 (Holy Thursday). 'Dear children! I thank you because you begin to think of the glory of God in your hearts. Today is the day when I wish to stop giving the messages because some individuals did not accept me. The parish has responded, and I wish to continue giving you the messages, like never before in history since the beginning of time. Thank you for your response to my call.'

April 5, 1985 (Good Friday). 'You the parishioners have a great and heavy cross. But do not be afraid to carry it. My Son is with you and He will help you.'

April 11, 1985. 'Dear children! Today I wish to say to everyone in the parish to pray in a special way for the enlightenment of the Holy Spirit. From today God wants to try the parish in a special way in order that He might strengthen it in faith. Thank you for your response to my call.'

April 18, 1985. 'Dear children! Today I wish to thank you for every opening of your hearts. Joy overwhelms me for every heart that opens to God, especially in the parish. Rejoice with me. Pray all the prayers for opening sinful hearts. I want this. God wants this through me. Thank you for your response to my call.'

April 25, 1985. 'Dear children! Today I want to tell you to begin work in your hearts as you work in the fields. Work and change your hearts so that the Spirit of God moves into your hearts. Thank you for your response to my call.'

May 2, 1985. 'Dear children! Today I invite you to prayer of the heart and not only by habit. Some are coming but do not move in prayer. Therefore I beg you as Mother: Pray that prayer prevails in your hearts in every moment. Thank you for your response to my call.'

May 9, 1985. 'Dear children! You do not know how many graces God is giving you. These days when the Holy Spirit is working in a special way, you do not want to advance. Your hearts are turned towards earthly things and you are occupied by them. Turn your hearts to prayer and ask the Holy Spirit to be poured on you. Thank you for your response to my call.'

May 16, 1985. 'Dear children! I am calling you to more attentive prayer and participation in the Mass. I want your Mass to be an experience of God. I want to say to the young especially: Be open to the Holy Spirit because God wants to draw you to Himself these days when Satan is active. Thank you for your response to my call.'

May 23, 1985. 'Dear children! Open your hearts to the Holy Spirit in a special way these days. The Holy Spirit is working in a special way through you. Open your hearts and give your lives to Jesus, so that He works through your hearts and strengthens you. Thank you for your response to my call.'

May 30, 1985. 'I am calling you again to prayer of the heart. Let prayer, dear children, be your everyday food. In a special way now when work in the fields is exhausting you, you cannot pray with your heart. Pray and then you will overcome every tiredness. Prayer will be your happiness and rest. Thank you for your response to my call.'

June 6, 1985. 'Dear children! These days people from all nations will be coming to the parish. And now I am calling you to love: first of all love your own household and then you will be able to accept and love all who are coming. Thank you for your response to my call.'

June 13, 1985. 'Dear children! Until the anniversary day I am calling you in the parish to pray more and let your prayer be a sign of your surrender to God. Dear children, I know about your tiredness. But you don't know how to surrender yourselves to me. These days surrender yourselves to me completely. Thank you for your response to my call.'

June 20, 1985. 'Dear children! I wish for you this Feast Day: Open your hearts to the Lord of all hearts. Give me all your feelings and all your problems. I wish to console you in all your temptations. I wish to fill you with the peace, joy and love of God. Thank you for your response to my call.'

June 25, 1985. 'Dear children! I ask you to ask everyone to pray the Rosary. With the Rosary you will overcome all the troubles which Satan is trying to inflict on the Catholic Church. Let all priests pray the Rosary. Give time to the Rosary.' Our Lady gave this message to Marija Pavlovic when she asked: 'Our Lady, what do you wish to say to priests?'

June 28, 1985. 'Dear children! Today I give you the messages through which I am calling you to humility. These days you have felt great joy because of all the people who were coming, and you have spoken about your experiences with love. Now I call you to continue in humility and with an open heart to speak to all those who are coming. Thank you for your response to my call.'

July 4, 1985. 'Dear children! I thank you for every sacrifice you have offered. And now I urge you to offer every sacrifice with love. I desire that you who are helpless will begin helping with trust and the Lord will give to you always in trust. Thank you for your response to my call.'

July 11, 1985. 'Dear children! I love the parish and with my mantle I protect it from every work of Satan. Pray that Satan flees from the parish and from every individual who comes to the parish. In that way you will be able to hear every call of God and answer it with your life. Thank you for your response to my call.'

July 18, 1985. 'Dear children! Today I beg you to put more blessed objects in your homes, and that everyone carry blessed objects. Let everything be blessed so that Satan will tempt you less because you are armed against him. Thank you for your response to my call.'

July 25, 1985. 'Dear children! I want to shepherd you but you do not want to obey my messages. Today I call you to obey my messages. Then you will be able to live everything that God tells me to tell you. Open yourselves to God and God will work through you and give you everything you need. Thank you for your response to my call.'

August 1, 1985. 'Dear children! I want to tell you that I have chosen this parish. I protect it, holding it in my hands like a fragile little flower that struggles for life. I beg you to give yourselves to me so that I can offer you clean and without sin as a gift to God. Satan has taken one part of the plan, and he wants to have it all. Pray that he does not succeed, because I desire to have you for myself to offer you to God. Thank you for your response to my call.'

August 8, 1985. 'Dear children! Today I call you to pray against Satan in a special way. Satan wants to work more now that you know he is active. Dear children, put on your armour against Satan; with rosaries in your hands you will conquer. Thank you for your response to my call.'

August 15, 1985. 'Dear children! Today I bless you, and I want to tell you that I love you. I appeal to you in this moment to live my messages. Today I bless you with a solemn blessing that the Almighty grants me to give. Thank you for your response to my call.'

August 29, 1985. 'Dear children! I call you to prayer especially now, when Satan wants to make use of the grapes of your vineyards. Pray that he does not succeed. Thank you for your response to my call.'

August 22, 1985. 'Dear children! Today I want to say to you that God wants to send you some tests over which you can prevail with prayer. God is testing you through the work of every day. Pray now that you overcome every temptation peacefully. By every trial that God tests you with, come to him more open, and approach him with love. Thank you for your response to my call.'

September 5, 1985 'Dear children! Today I thank you for all your prayers. Keep on praying so that Satan will stay far away from this place. Dear children, the plan of Satan has failed. Pray that everything God plans for this village becomes reality. In a special way I want to thank the young people for all the sacrifices they have offered. Thank you for your response to my call.'

September 12, 1985. 'Dear children! I want to ask you that in these days you put the cross in the centre. Pray in a special way before the cross; many graces come from the cross. Make a special consecration to the holy cross in your homes. Promise that you will not offend Jesus nor offend against the cross, and that you will not blaspheme. Thank you for your response to my call.'

September 20, 1985. 'Dear children! Today I ask you to live in humility all the messages I give you. Dear children, do not become proud living the messages, saying in your hearts, "I live the messages!" If you bear the messages in your heart and if you live them, then everyone will feel it and there will be no need for words; words are used only by those who do not listen. It is not necessary for you to speak with words. For you dear children it is necessary only to live the messages and to witness with your lives. Thank you for your response to my call.'

September 26, 1985. 'Dear children! I thank you for all your prayers. Thank you for all the sacrifices. I wish to tell you, dear children, to renew living the messages that I have given you. In particular, live the messages regarding fasting, because your fasting gives me joy. And so you will attain the fulfilment of all the plans that God has for you here in Medjugorje. Thank you for your response to my call.'

October 3, 1985. 'Dear children! I ask you to give thanks to God for all the graces that He gives you. Give thanks to God for all the fruits of His grace, and praise Him. Dear children, learn how to give thanks for little things, and then you will be able to give thanks for great things. Thank you for your response to my call.'

October 10, 1985. 'Dear children! Again today I want to call you to live out my messages in the parish. I want to call especially the young persons of the parish; I love this parish so much. Dear children, if you live my messages, you live the seed of holiness. As your mother, I want to call all of you to holiness so that you can lead others to holiness — because you are like a mirror for other people. Thank you for responding to my call.'

October 17, 1985. 'Dear children! Everything has its time. Today I invite you to begin working on your hearts. All the work in the fields is finished. You found the time to clean out the most abandoned places, but you have neglected your hearts. Work hard and clean up every part of your heart with love. Thank you for responding to my message.'

October 24, 1985. 'Dear children! I want to dress you from day to day in holiness, goodness, obedience, and the love of God, so that from day to day you can be more beautiful and better prepared for your Lord. Dear children, listen to my messages and live them. I desire to lead you! Thank you for responding to my call.'

October 31, 1985. 'Dear children! Today I want to call you to work in the Church. I love all of you and I want all of you to work as much as you can. I know, dear children, that you can but you do not want to because you feel too insignificant and unworthy for such things. You must be courageous and enrich the Church and Jesus with little flowers so that all can be pleased. Thank you for your response to my call.'

November 7, 1985. 'Dear children! I call you to love — love towards your fellow people, and love towards those from whom evil comes to you. And so through love you will be able to discern the intentions of hearts. Pray and love, dear children! With love you can do even what you think is impossible. Thank you for your response to my call.'

November 14, 1985. 'Dear children! I your mother love you and wish to urge you to prayer. I am tireless, dear children, and I call you even when you are far away from my heart. I feel pain for everyone who has gone astray. But I am a mother, and I forgive easily; and I rejoice over every child who comes back to me! Thank you for your response to my call.'

November 21, 1985. 'I wish to tell you that this time is special for you who belong to the parish. In the summer you say that you have a lot of work to do. Now there is no work in the fields; work on yourselves personally!

Come to the Mass, because this time has been given to you. Dear children, many of you come regularly in spite of bad weather because they love me and they want to show their love in a special way. I ask you to show me your love by coming to the Mass, and the Lord will reward you abundantly. Thank you for responding to my call.'

November 28, 1985. 'Dear children! I want to give thanks to all for all that they have done for me, especially the young people. I beg you, dear children, to pray with conscious attention, and in prayer you will know the majesty of God. Thank you for your response to my call.'

December 5, 1985. 'Dear children! I call you to prepare yourselves for Christmas by penance, prayer, and works of charity. Do not look at the material, because then you will not be able to experience Christmas.'

December 12, 1985. 'Dear children! For Christmas I invite you to give glory to Jesus together with me. I will give Him to you in a special way on that day, and I invite you on that day to give glory and praise with me to Jesus at His birth. Dear children, pray more on that day, and think more about Jesus. Thank you for responding to my call.'

December 19, 1985. 'Dear children! Today I want to invite you to love your neighbour. If you love your neighbour you will experience Jesus more, especially on Christmas day. God will give you great gifts if you abandon yourselves to him. I want to give to mothers in particular on Christmas day my special maternal blessing. And Jesus will bless the others with His blessing. Thank you for responding to my call.'

December 26, 1985. 'Dear children! I want to thank all of you who have listened to my messages, and who have lived on Christmas day what I told you. I want to guide you, purified now from your sins, from now on to go forward in love. Abandon your hearts to me. Thank you for responding to my call.'

January 2, 1986. 'Dear children! I invite you to decide completely for God. I beg you, dear children, to surrender yourselves completely and you will be able to live everything I say to you. It will not be difficult for you to surrender yourselves completely to God. Thank you for responding to my call.'

January 9, 1986. 'Dear children! I invite you to help Jesus through prayer to fulfil all the plans that he has for this parish. Offer your sacrifices to Jesus in order that all he has planned may be fulfilled and that Satan can do nothing. Thank you for your response to my call.'

January 16, 1986. 'Dear children! Today I invite you to pray. I need your prayer so much in order that God may be glorified through all of you. Dear children, I beg you to listen and to live your mother's call, because I am calling only by reason of my love for you, so that I can help you. Thank you for your response to my call.'

January 23, 1986. Dear children! Again I invite you to prayer of the heart. If you pray in your heart, dear children, the ice-cold hearts of your brothers and sisters will melt, and every barrier will disappear. Conversion will be easily achieved by those who want it. You must intercede for the gift of conversion for your neighbour. Thank you for your response to my call.'

January 30, 1986. 'Dear children! Today I invite all of you to pray in order that God's plans with you, and all that God wants through you, may be realised. Help others to be converted, especially those who come to Medjugorje. Dear children, do not allow Satan to reign in your hearts. Do not be an image of Satan, but my image. I am calling you to pray so that you may be witnesses of my presence. God cannot fulfil His will without you. God gave everyone free will, and it is up to you to be disposed. Thank you for responding to my call.'

February 6, 1986. 'Dear children! This parish chosen by me is special, and is different from others. And I am offering great graces to all who are praying from their hearts. Dear children, I am giving my messages first of all to the parish, and then to all others. The messages should be accepted first of all by you and then by others. You will be responsible to me and to my Son Jesus. Thank you for responding to my call.'

February 13, 1986. 'Dear children! This Lent is a special incentive for you to change. Start from this moment. Turn off the television and renounce other things which are useless. Dear children, I am calling you individually to conversion. This time is for you. Thank you for your response to my call.'

February 20, 1986. 'Dear children! The second message for Lent is: you must renew your prayer before the cross. Dear children, I offer you special graces, and Jesus gives you special gifts from the cross. Accept them and live them. Meditate on the passion of Jesus, and be united with Jesus in your lives.'

February 27, 1986. 'Dear children! Live the messages I am giving you in humbleness. Thank you for your response to my call.'

March 6, 1986. 'Dear children! Today I am calling you to open yourselves more to God, so that He can work through you. For as much as you open yourselves, you will receive the fruits from it. I wish to call you again to prayer. Thank you for your response to my call.'

March 13, 1986. 'Dear children! Today I am calling you to live this Lent with your little sacrifices. Thank you for every sacrifice you have brought me. Dear children, live in such a way, continuously, and with love, help me to bring the offering. For that, God will reward you. Thank you for your response to my call.'

March 20, 1986. 'Dear children! I am calling you to an active approach to prayer. You wish to live everything I am telling you, but you do not have results from your efforts because you do not pray. Dear children, I beg you, open yourselves and begin to pray. Prayer will be a joy. If you begin, it will not be boring because you will pray out of pure joy. Thank you for your response to my call.'

March 27, 1986. 'Dear children! I wish to thank you for your sacrifices and I invite you to the greatest sacrifice, the sacrifice of love. Without love, you are not able to accept me or my Son. Without love, you cannot speak of your experiences to others. That is why I invite you, dear children, to begin to live the love within yourselves. Thank you for your response to my call.'

April 3, 1986. 'Dear children! I wish to call you to live the Holy Mass. There are many of you who have experienced the beauty of the Holy Mass, but there are some who come unwillingly. I have chosen you, dear children, and Jesus is giving you His graces in the Holy Mass. Therefore, live consciously the Holy Mass. Let every coming to Holy Mass be joyful. With love, come and accept Holy Mass. Thank you for your response to my call.'

April 10, 1986. 'Dear children! I wish to call you to grow in love. A flower cannot grow without water. Neither can you grow, dear children, without God's blessing. You should seek God's blessing from day to day so that you may grow normally and do everything with God. Thank you for your response to my call.'

April 17, 1986. 'Dear children! You are preoccupied with material things, and in the material you lose everything that God wants to give you. I am inviting you, dear children, to pray for the gifts of the Holy Spirit which you need so as to witness to my presence and all that I am giving you. Dear children, surrender yourselves to me so that I can lead you completely. Do not preoccupy yourselves with material things. Thank you for your response to my call.'

April 24, 1986. 'Dear children! Today I am calling you to pray. Dear children, you are forgetting that you are all important. The elderly are especially important in the family. Urge them to pray. Let the young people be an example to the others. Let them witness to Jesus by their lives. Dear children, I beg you, start changing yourselves through prayer and you will know what to do. Thank you for your response to my call.'

May 1, 1986. 'Dear children! I beg you to start changing your life in the family. Let the family be a unitive flower that I wish to give to Jesus. Dear children, let every family be active in prayer. I wish that the fruits would be seen in the family one day. Only in that way as petals will I give you to Jesus, in fulfilment of God's plan. Thank you for your response to my call.'

May 8, 1986. Dear children! You are responsible for the messages. The source of grace is here, but you, dear children, are the vessels transmitting the gifts. Therefore, dear children, I am calling you to work with responsibility. Everybody will be responsible according to his own measure. Dear children, I am calling you to give the gifts to others with love and not to keep them to yourselves. Thank you for your response to my call.'

May 15, 1986. 'Dear children! Today I am calling you to give me your heart so I can change it to be like mine. You are asking yourselves, dear children, why you cannot respond to what I am seeking from you. You cannot because you have not given me your heart so I can change it. You are speaking but not acting. I call you to do everything I tell you. In that way I will be with you. Thank you for your response to my call.'

May 22, 1986. 'Dear children! Today I will give you my love. You do not know, dear children, how great is my love, and you do not know how to accept it. In different ways, I wish to show it, but you, dear children, do not recognise it. You do not understand my words by your heart and so you are not able to comprehend my love. Dear children, accept me in your lives and so you will be able to accept all I am saying to you and all I am calling you for. Thank you for your response to my call.'

May 29, 1986. 'Dear children! Today I am calling you to a life of love towards God and your neighbour. Without love, dear children, you cannot do anything. Therefore, dear children, I am calling you to live in mutual love. Only in that way you will love me and accept everyone around you coming to your parish. Everyone will feel my love through you. Therefore, today I beg you to start loving with the burning love with which I love you. Thank you for your response to my call.'

June 5, 1986. 'Dear children! Today I am calling you to decide if you wish to live the messages I am giving you. I wish you to be active in living the messages. Especially, dear children, I desire you to be the reflection of

Jesus who enlightens this unfaithful world which is walking in darkness. I wish that all of you be a light to all and to witness in the light. Dear children, you are not called to darkness, you are called to light. Therefore, live the light with your life. Thank you for your response to my call.'

June 12, 1986. 'Dear children! Today I am calling you to begin to pray the Rosary with a living faith. That way I will be able to help you. You, dear children, want to receive graces, but you do not pray. I cannot help you because you do not want to move. Dear children, I am calling you to pray the Rosary and that the Rosary should be your commitment which you will pray with joy. That way you will understand why I am such a long time with you. I want to teach you to pray. Thank you for your response to my call.'

June 19, 1986. 'Dear children! In these days my Lord allowed me to intercede for more graces for you. Therefore, dear children, I want to urge you once again to pray without ceasing and in this way I will give you that joy which the Lord gives me. With these graces, dear children, I want your sufferings to be a joy. I am your Mother and I want to help you. Thank you for your response to my call.'

June 29, 1986. 'Dear children! God allowed me to bring about this oasis of peace. I want to invite you to guard it and let the oasis remain pure always. There are those who destroy peace and prayer by their carelessness. I am calling you to witness and by your life to preserve peace. Thank you for your response to my call.'

July 3, 1986. 'Dear children! Today I am calling you all to prayer. Without prayer, dear children, you cannot feel either God or me or the graces I am giving you. Therefore, I am asking that the beginning and end of every day always be prayer. Dear children, I wish to lead you in prayer from day to day, but you cannot grow because you do not want. I am calling you, dear children, that prayer be in the first place. Thank you for your response to my call.'

July 10, 1986. 'Dear children! Today I am calling you to holiness. Without holiness you cannot live. Therefore, overcome every sin with love. Overcome every difficulty which arises with love. Dear children, I beg you, live love within yourselves. Thank you for your response to my call.'

July 17, 1986. 'Dear children! Today I am calling you to reflect upon why I am with you for this length of time. I am a mediator between you and God. Therefore, dear children, I am calling you to live out of love everything that God wants from you. For that reason, dear children, live all the messages I am giving in humbleness. Thank you for your response to my call.'

July 24, 1986. 'Dear children! I rejoice because of all of you who are on the way to holiness, and I beg you — help those who do not know how to live in holiness by your own testimony. Therefore, dear children, let your family be a place where holiness is born. Help everyone to live in holiness, especially your own family. Thank you for your response to my call.'

July 31, 1986. 'Dear children! Hate gives birth to divisions and does not see anybody or anything. I invite you to carry unity and peace always. Especially, dear children, act with love in the place where you live. Let your only tool always be love. With love turn everything to good that Satan wants to destroy and take to himself. Only in this way will you be completely mine and I will be able to help you. Thank you for your response to my call.'

August 7, 1986. 'Dear children! You know I promised you an oasis of peace here. But you are not aware that around every oasis is a desert where Satan is lurking and he wants to tempt each one of you. Dear children, only by prayer are you able to overcome every influence of Satan in your place. I am with you but I cannot take away your free will. Thank you for your response to my call.'

August 14, 1986. 'Dear children! I am inviting you that your prayer becomes a joy of encounter with the Lord. I cannot guide you as long as you do not experience the joy of prayer. More and more I want to guide you from day to day in prayer, but I do not want to force you. Thank you for your response to my call.'

August 21, 1986. 'Dear children! I thank you for the love you are showing me. You know, dear children, I love you immeasurably, and from day to day I pray to the Lord to help you to understand the love which I am showing you. Therefore, dear children, pray, pray, pray. Thank you for your response to my call.'

August 28, 1986. 'Dear children! I call you to be a picture to everyone in everything, especially in prayer and witnessing. Dear children, I cannot help the world without you. I want you to co-operate with me in everything, even in the smallest things. Therefore, dear children, help me by your prayer from your heart and by surrendering to me completely. In that way I will be able to teach you and lead you on this road which I began with you. Thank you for your response to my call.'

September 4, 1986. 'Dear children! Today again I am calling you to prayer and fasting. You know, dear children, that with your help I can do everything and force Satan not to seduce people to evil, and to remove him from this place. Satan, dear children, watches for every individual. He wants particularly to bring confusion to every one of you. Therefore, dear children, I ask that your every day becomes prayer and complete surrender to God. Thank you for your response to my call.'

September 11, 1986. 'Dear children! For these days while you are joyfully celebrating the cross, I desire that your cross also is a joy for you. Especially, dear children, pray that you are able to accept illness and suffering with love, like Jesus accepted them. Only in that way, with joy, will I be able to give you the graces and healings which Jesus allows me. Thank you for your response to my call.'

September 18, 1986. 'Dear children! Today again I am grateful for everything that you have done for me in these days. Especially, dear children, I thank you in the name of Jesus for the sacrifices you offered in this last week. Dear children, you are forgetting that I want sacrifices from you to help you and to banish Satan. Therefore I am calling you again to offer sacrifices, with a special reverence towards God. Thank you for your response to my call.'

September 25, 1986. 'Dear children! Through your own peace, I am calling you to help others to see and to start searching for peace. You are, dear children, at peace, and you cannot comprehend absence of peace. Therefore I am calling you, so that through your prayer and your life you help to destroy everything evil in people, and uncover the deceptions that Satan uses. Pray for truth to prevail in every heart. Thank you for your response to my call.'

October 2, 1986. 'Dear children! Today again I invite you to prayer. You dear children will not be able to understand the value of prayer until you say to yourselves: "Now it is time to pray; now nothing else is important; now for me no person is as important as God." Dear children, dedicate yourselves to prayer with particular love, so that God can give you graces. Thank you for your response to my call.'

October 9, 1986. 'Dear children! You know that I desire to lead you on the way of holiness. However, I do not want to force you, to be holy by force. I want each of you to help yourself and me by little sacrifices; in that way I can guide you, and you, day by day, will come closer to holiness. However, dear children, I do not want to compel you to live my messages; but the length of time during which I have been with you is a sign that I love you immensely and desire each one of you to become holy. Thank you for your response to my call.'

October 16, 1986. 'Dear children! Today again I want to show you how much I love you; therefore it saddens me not to be able to help each of you to understand my love. Therefore, dear children, I invite you to prayer and to total abandonment to God, because Satan desires to conquer you in daily things and to take first place in your lives. Because of this, dear children, pray constantly. Thank you for your response to my call.'

October 23, 1986. 'Dear children! Today again I invite you to pray; in particular, dear children, I invite you to pray for peace. Without your prayers, dear children, I cannot possibly help you to realise the mission given to me by the Lord for you. Therefore, dear children, pray; because in praying you will obtain the peace which the Lord is giving to you. Thank you for your response to my call.'

October 30, 1986. 'Dear children! I desire again today to invite you to receive, seriously, the messages which I give you. Dear children, for you I have stayed so long, to help you to put into practice the messages which I give you. Therefore, dear children, live with love for me, the messages I give you. Thank you for your response to my call.'

November 6, 1986. 'Dear children! Today I ask you to pray daily for the souls in purgatory. Prayer and grace are needed for every soul to reach the love of God. In so doing, dear children, you acquire new intercessors who will help you in life to understand that all earthly things are unimportant for you; that you should hold on only to heaven. Therefore, dear children, pray unceasingly. In that way you will help yourself and others to whom your prayer will bring joy. Thank you for your response to my call.'

November 13, 1986. 'Dear children! Today I ask you to pray with your whole heart, and to change your life day by day. I especially ask you, dear children, to begin to live in a holy way, with prayers and sacrifices. Because I desire that every one of you who has been in this fountain, or near to this fountain of grace, will reach heaven by the special gift which has been given to me, that is, holiness. Therefore, dear children, pray, and change your lives towards holiness. I shall always be close to you. Thank you for your response to my call.'

November 20, 1986. 'Dear children! Today I invite you to live, and to follow with special love, all the messages I give you. Dear children, God does not want you to be tepid and indecisive, but he wants you to be completely abandoned to him. You know that I love you and that I desire every good for you. Therefore, dear children, you decide, too, to live in love and day by day to know the love of God. Dear children, decide for love, so that love reigns in all; not human love, however, but divine. Thank you for your response to my call.'

November 27, 1986. 'Dear children! Today I invite you to consecrate your life to me, with love. That way I can guide you with love. I love you dear children, with a special love, and I want to lead all to God in heaven. I want you to understand that this life lasts a little while compared to that of heaven; therefore, dear children, decide today anew for God; only so can I show you how dear you are to me, and how much I desire all of you to be saved and to be with me in heaven. Thank you for your response to my call.'

December 4, 1986. 'Dear children! Today I ask you to prepare your hearts for these days in which the Lord desires in a particular way to cleanse all the sins of your past. Dear children, you cannot do it alone; therefore I am here to help you. Pray, dear children, only so you can know all the evil that is in you and offer it to the Lord in such a way that the Lord may purify your hearts of everything. Therefore, dear children, pray without ceasing, and prepare your hearts by penance and fasting. Thank you for your response to my call.'

December 11, 1986. 'Dear children! In a particular way I invite you at this time to pray to be able to live the experience of the joy of the meeting with the new born Jesus. I desire, dear children, that you live these days as I live them, in joy. I wish to guide you, and to show you the joy to which I want to lead each one of you. Therefore, dear children, .pray, and abandon yourselves totally to me. Thank you for your response to my call.'

December 18, 1986. 'Dear children! Anew today I want to invite you to prayer. When you pray you are so much more beautiful; like flowers which after snow show all their beauty, and all their colours become indescribable. So also you, dear children, after prayer, show in God's sight all the beauty which makes you more dear to him. For this reason, dear children, pray and offer your inmost heart to the Lord, because he makes of you a harmonious and beautiful heavenly flower. Thank you for hearing my call.'

December 25, 1986. 'Dear children! Again today I bless the Lord for all that he is doing for me, in a particular way for the gift of being able to be with you today. Dear children, in these days the Father offers particular graces to all those who open their hearts. I bless you and desire that you too, dear children, know these graces and place all at God's disposal, so that God may be glorified through you. I follow your steps attentively. Thank you for your response to my call.'

January 1, 1987. 'Dear children! Today I want to invite all of you to live, in the new year, all the messages I give you. Dear children, know that I am beside you to enable you to learn how to walk on the road of holiness. Therefore, dear children, pray unceasingly, and live all the messages which I give you, because I do all this with great love towards God and towards you. Thank you for your response to my call.'

January 8, 1987. 'Dear children! I want to thank you for every response to the messages, especially, dear children, I thank you for all the sacrifices and the prayers which you have offered me. Dear children, I desire from now on not to give the messages every Thursday, but on the 25th of every month. The time has come in which all is complete which my Lord has desired. From today I will give fewer messages, but I am with you. Therefore, dear children, I beg you: listen to my messages and live them; that way I can guide you. Dear children, thank you for having responded to my call.'

January 25, 1987. 'Dear children! Today I wish to invite you to begin, all of you, from today, to live a new life. Dear children, I want you to understand that God has chosen each one of you to use you in his great plan for the salvation of humanity. You cannot understand how great your role is in God's project. Therefore, dear children, pray, so that in prayer you may understand God's plan for you. I am with you so that you may realise it fully. Thank you for responding to my call.'

• *The great cross on the hill.*

• *Marija and Jakov...continuing to see Our Lady.*

• *Ivanka marries Raiko Elez on December 28, 1986.*

Update — February 1987

by Lucy Rooney

Interest in Medjugorje grows, even among people who at first scorned the idea of the Mother of God appearing in our time as she did at Lourdes and Fatima: 'I'm not into apparitions,' they said. But television documentaries have left both viewers and film-makers touched, and saying 'Something is going on there'. The comportment of the six young people during these five years has been the greatest proof of the validity of their claims.

Marija, Vicka and Jakov continue to see Our Lady daily. Ivan sees her when he is on leave from his army base. Ivanka, who will be 21 in April, was married on December 28 to Raiko Elez, of Medjugorje.

In October 1986, Cardinal Ratzinger, as Prefect of the Congregation for the Doctrine of the Faith, which had taken the investigation of the Medjugorje events out of the hands of the local bishop, Bishop Zanic, asked the Yugoslav Bishops' Conference to set up a national commission to continue the study of the case. In setting up the new national commission, Cardinal Franjo Kuharic of Zagreb, as president of the Bishops' Conference, with Bishop Zanic as local ordinary, issued a statement reminding the faithful of the usual prudence to be observed until the Church judges the matter. They continued: 'It is therefore not permissible to organise pilgrimages or other manifestations *motivated by attributing a supernatural character to the facts of Medjugorje*. Legitimate devotion to the Madonna, recommended by the Church, must conform to the directives of the magisterium.' Archbishop Frane Franic of Split, president of the Yugoslav Bishops' Conference's Commission for the Doctrine of the Faith, interviewed by the Milan *Association Regina della Pace*, said comments in the press subsequent to the statement 'completely distorted' the Yugoslav bishops' intention, which he said was that all might make pilgrimages, private or organised, bishops and cardinals too, *for motives of devotion, formation, conversion.* Only *official* pilgrimages, led by a bishop of a diocese, were prohibited, as applying acceptance by the Church of the events as supernatural. Legitimate devotion would not preempt the Church's eventual judgment.

On 24 January 1987, Pope John Paul received the bishops of Triveneto (Italy) for their *ad limina* visit. One of them asked: 'How are we to act with regard to Medjugorje?' The Pope replied: 'I'm astonished at this question. Aren't you aware of the marvellous fruits it is producing?'

It is perhaps the Medjugorje events that have led Pope John Paul to declare a Marian year from Pentecost 1987. Meanwhile, on 28 January 1987, Our Lady spoke to Mirjana at Sarajevo, and seemed to sum up the purpose of her intervention in our times:

Message Given To Mirjana at
Sarajevo, 28 January, 1987.

Dear children, I have come to you to lead you to purity of soul, and so to God.

How have you listened to me? At the beginning: without believing, in fear, and with distrust towards the girls and boys I have chosen. Then most of you welcomed me in your hearts, and began to put into practice my motherly requests. But, however, this has not lasted very long.

Wherever I come, and with me my Son, Satan arrives too. Without being aware of it, you have allowed him to take the upper hand in you; he dominates you. At times you have understood that some of the things you do are not from God, but you quickly quell this feeling.

Don't allow this my children! Dry the tears on my face which pour down, seeing your behaviour. Look around you!

Take time to come to your God in church. Come to your Father's house.

Take time to get together in your family to implore grace from God.

Remember your dead. Give them joy with the celebration of the Mass.

Don't look with disdain at the poor who ask you for a crust of bread. Don't send them away from your plentiful table. Help them! And then God will help you. Perhaps the blessing, which he [the poor person] gives you in place of thanks, will come about, perhaps God will hear it.

You my children have forgotten these things. And Satan has influenced you also in this.

Don't let him, pray with me! Don't deceive yourselves, thinking: 'I am good, but my brother and sister beside me are worth nothing.' This is not right.

I, as your Mother, love you, and therefore I admonish you.

There are secrets, my sons and daughters, which will remain unknown; but by the time you know it will be too late.

Return to prayer. Nothing is more important. I want the Lord to allow me to make clear, even a little, these secrets; but already the graces he offers you are too much.

Reflect on how much you offer him. When did you last give something up, for the Lord?

I don't want to reproach you further, I want instead to invite you once again to prayer, to fasting, to penance.

If with fasting you desire to obtain grace from God, no one should know that you are fasting.

If with a gift to a poor person you want to receive grace from God, nobody should know of it, except you and the Lord.

Listen to me my children, reflect in prayer on my message.